An Aussie Christmas Carol

Also by Kel Richards
from Strand Publishing

Aussie Yarns
Aussie Pilgrim's Progress

An Aussie Christmas Carol

Charles Dickens' immortal tale
retold as an Aussie bush yarn by

Kel Richards

STRAND PUBLISHING

Sydney

An Aussie Christmas Carol
Copyright © 2007 Kel Richards

First published 2007 by Strand Publishing

ISBN 978 1 921 20213 1

Distributed in Australia by:
Family Reading Publications
B100 Ring Road
Ballarat Victoria 3352
Phone: 03 5334 3244
Fax: 03 5334 3299
Email: info@familyreading.com.au

Gary Allen Pty Ltd
www.garyallen.com.au
Phone: (02) 9725 2933
Email: sales@garyallen.com.au

Edited by Owen Salter
Cover design by Joy Lankshear
Typeset by Midland Typesetters, Australia
Printed in Australia by McPherson's Printing Group

Contents

The First Verse: Marley's Ghost

Jack Marley was dead. He was dead and buried in the little cemetery at the end of the main street in the small outback town of Dandaloo. The town doctor had signed the death certificate. The town minister had conducted the funeral. The town carpenter had nailed Jack Marley into a plain, wooden coffin—and old Jack hadn't once hammered on the lid and yelled to be let out. So there could be no doubt about it: Jack Marley was dead.

He was as dead as the hopes of a punter when the favourite runs last in the Melbourne Cup. He was as dead as Dandaloo Creek in the middle of summer, when it's nothing but a dried-up gully. He was as dead as the big blue-black blowflies stuck to the fly paper in the Dandaloo Pub. He was as dead as the brown snake Bluey Grimes chopped in half with his mattock when he was digging Marley's grave. There was no doubt about it: Jack Marley was dead.

Did Ted Scrooge know he was dead? Of course he did. The faded sign across the front of the old weatherboard office said: *Scrooge and Marley—Stock and Station Agents*. And Scrooge and Marley had been partners for as long as anyone could remember. The old blokes reckoned they could recall when Banjo Paterson rode through town and described Dandaloo as

> *A township where life's total sum*
> *Is sleep, diversified with rum.*

But even those old blokes couldn't remember when Scrooge and Marley first went into partnership. It was that long ago.

When Marley had made his will, having no wife or kids he'd left everything to Scrooge. And Scrooge, being in the same solitary position in life, had done the same. The old blokes reckoned that was the only thing that kept the partnership together: they were both hanging on to see who'd die first.

In the end Scrooge had the pleasure of seeing Marley win the race to the cemetery. So Marley's will, now yellow with age, was dug out of the safe of the town solicitor, and Scrooge was appointed sole executor and sole heir.

Ted Scrooge certainly knew that Jack Marley was dead—and he wasn't exactly cut up about it, either. He closed the office for ten minutes for Marley's funeral and then opened it straight up again.

There had only been three people at the graveside ceremony: Ted Scrooge, the town minister and Bluey Grimes, who was leaning on his shovel waiting to fill in the hole. There were also several of the town dogs, who turned up out of curiosity. There wasn't much to do in Dandaloo and a funeral was as good as anything to help pass the time. So little happened in

Dandaloo that when a car got a tank filled with petrol, the younger dogs would gather at the petrol station to watch the numbers tick over on the pump. The older dogs just lay in the sun—they'd seen it all before.

After the funeral several of the dogs followed Ted Scrooge down the main street, back to the office of *Scrooge and Marley—Stock and Station Agents*. The younger dogs hoped he might toss them a scrap. But the older dogs didn't lift their heads from their paws. They just thought, 'It's Scrooge, you boof-heads! You won't get anything out of him!'

Scrooge never painted out Marley's name on the front of the old weatherboard office. He just let the paint slowly fade in the blistering sun. But the words *Scrooge and Marley* could still be faintly read. Sometimes a visitor to town would come to the office and address him as 'Mr Scrooge' and some-times as 'Mr Marley'. Scrooge didn't mind. He answered to both names—as long as they had money to spend. It was all the same to him.

As far as Ted Scrooge was concerned, it was all about the money. Scrooge was out for every dollar he could get. And every dollar he ever got he stuffed into his bank account. In it went—and it never came out. Scrooge was famous for being tight-fisted. Everyone said he had deep pockets and short arms.

When he visited the Big Smoke, someone might be bold enough to ask Scrooge for a tip. He'd turn around and snarl, 'Don't throw yer money away!' And when they looked puzzled he'd add, 'That's my tip for you . . . and it's the best tip you'll ever get.'

Back in Dandaloo the daily grind of business continued. Scrooge bought as low as he could and sold as high as he could. In winter the rains would come and the creek would rise, but Scrooge just sat at his desk doing business. In summer the heat would beat down, and the dry, red dust would swirl around and get into everything, but it made no difference to Scrooge, who sat at his desk and kept doing business.

If you wanted to buy or sell a property or a herd in the district then you had to do business with Scrooge. He was the only stock and station agent for miles around, and he represented the big dealers in Sydney, Melbourne, Brisbane and Adelaide. All the buying and selling in Dandaloo was done by Scrooge, or through Scrooge. But you kept your business dealings with him as short as possible—in order to keep the unpleasantness of dealing with Scrooge as short as possible.

When he walked home in the gathering gloom each evening, no swaggie ever stopped Scrooge and asked for a handout. They took one look at his squinting, shrivelled up face and knew it was a bad idea. No one ever stopped him in the street to say, 'G'day,' and have a yarn. No little old lady waddling out of Charley Carlton's butcher's shop ever smiled at Scrooge and said, 'How are you today, Ted?' There wasn't a big population in Dandaloo, and those who lived there knew to keep out of Scrooge's way.

The town butcher was always good for a joke; the town publican was always good for a tip on the races; the town minister was always good for a friendly word; and Scrooge was always good for a snarl and a snap. He was known as the town grump, and his office was nicknamed 'the growlery'.

Then one particularly blazing hot summer day

saw the town in a state of cheerful (if sweaty and exhausted) anticipation, for it was Christmas Eve.

Down the main street, clouds of that red dust were being carried along by a swirling, hot wind. As a customer left a shop the shopkeeper would shout after them, 'Shut the door!' Bluey Grimes was seen chasing his battered old Akubra down the street, and after just a few feet giving up the chase as a bad idea and staggering into the Dandaloo Pub for a cold beer.

The housewives of the town dared not hang out any wet washing, knowing it would come in caked with dust and ten times dirtier than before it was washed. The town dogs were crawling into any little bit of shade they could find (and they couldn't find much).

And even when doors were closed, the hot, fine dust came leaking in through keyholes and blowing in under doors. Old air conditioners were clanking, and banging and grinding to a halt—defeated by the effort of cooling such searing, dry air and crunching through such fine, gritty dust. In offices and shops men were taking off their shirts and working in their blue singlets, while women splashed their hot faces with water and tried to keep on going.

Ted Scrooge sat in the front office of *Scrooge and Marley—Stock and Station Agents*. He kept his inner door open so that he could keep one eye on the solitary clerk he employed, who worked in a windowless inner room. The clerk sat, dripping with sweat, in that oven of a room (for Scrooge wouldn't let him take his shirt off), doing the accounts and looking up every so often at the small electric fan that stood in the corner. He wanted to turn it on, but Scrooge was careful to keep the electricity bill as low as possible. The clerk had started to ask about the fan once already on that Christmas Eve, but Scrooge's only response had been a growl.

So the clerk sat looking at the fan in the corner, trying to imagine what it would be like to feel a current of air blowing gently over his face. He failed. He didn't have much imagination.

Just then the front door of the office burst open, and a voice cried out, 'Merry Christmas, Uncle Ted! God bless you, and Merry Christmas!' The voice belonged to Scrooge's nephew, who stood in the doorway wearing shorts and a T-shirt and heavy farm boots and, most of all, a huge grin.

'Shut the blasted door!' snapped Scrooge, 'before we all choke on that stinking dust!'

'Sorry, Uncle Ted,' murmured the nephew in a contrite voice as he stepped inside and pulled the door closed. 'Anyway, it's Christmas time—ignore the dust. Merry Christmas, Uncle Ted!' he added, regaining his good humour.

'Bah!' snarled Scrooge. 'Christmas! Tommyrot! Humbug!'

'What have you got against Christmas, Uncle Ted?' said Scrooge's nephew with a grin as he threw himself into a cane chair. 'You've got no reason to be as mad as a cut snake. It's Christmas time!'

'It's Christmas rubbish,' grumbled his uncle.

'Surely you don't mean that?'

'I do. Merry Christmas indeed,' sneered Scrooge. 'Merry codswallop! Whaddaya reckon *you've* got to be merry about? Are you rich, eh? Nah, of course not! Stop bunging on an act.'

'For a start it's not an act, Uncle Ted,' replied the

nephew with a laugh. 'I know how to have a good time at Christmas. On top of which—what right have *you* got to be miserable? If you reckon you gotta be rich to be happy, well, you oughta be the happiest bloke in town.'

'Bulldust!' snarled Scrooge—that being the cleverest, wittiest, most intellectual argument he could think of on the spot. He followed it with a low, growling 'Bah!' He paused, and then he said a second time, 'Bah!'

'That just makes you sound like a sick sheep,' said his nephew with a laugh. 'Come on—cheer up, Uncle Ted.'

'How can I cheer up when I live in a world of dills and drongos? Empty-headed numbskulls who go around grinning like lunatics and all repeating, "Have a merry Christmas and God bless." Bah! They might as well say, "Have a plastic Christmas and drop dead" for all it means!'

'But ... but ... but ...' stuttered his nephew, trying to think of what to say.

'What *is* Christmas after all?' Scrooge continued. 'It's a time for buying presents you can't afford to give to people you don't like, and sending Christmas cards in bad taste to people you almost never see, and running up credit card bills you'll struggle to pay, and eating too much and drinking too much, and watching the cricket with a hangover on Boxing Day. That's all Christmas is. And then you'll spend the next month trying to lose all the weight you put on over Christmas, and remembering how the family argued about politics all through Christmas dinner! Don't you "Merry Christmas" me!'

'Aw, fair go, Uncle Ted,' pleaded his nephew.

But Scrooge had a head of steam up now and wasn't about to stop. 'Listen, young fellah, there are idiots who'll go around yelling "Merry Christmas" to people they barely know, and then on Christmas Day they'll eat hot turkey and hot Christmas pudding—in the middle of a hot summer in the bush! Christmas is just an annual outbreak of mass insanity. That's all!'

His nephew opened his mouth like a goldfish gasping for air (or water, I suppose, which would please a goldfish more than air). Anyway, he gasped, and couldn't quite find the words to reply.

'You keep Christmas your way, and I'll keep it my way,' Scrooge concluded.

'Keep it?' said his nephew at last. 'But you don't keep it.'

'Yes I do,' insisted Scrooge. 'I keep it well away from me. So you can keep your "Merry Christmases" to yourself. Ignoring Christmas has never done me any harm, and all your "Merry Christmases" added together have never done you any good.'

'Well,' said his nephew thoughtfully, 'I certainly haven't profited from Christmas in the way that you count profit. But I'm sure I've always thought of Christmas as a time of family get-togethers. And it's a time when the whole town comes to the park for Carols by Candlelight. And just about everyone goes to church on Christmas Day, and we sing those great old Christmas carols and hear the Christmas story told again. And we remember the Founder of the Feast—the baby born in Bethlehem: God's great and good invasion of our world. And hearts are lifted and everyone is encouraged. We don't make a dollar out of it, but somehow, at least for a little while, we all like each other just a bit more, and we feel that we can carry on for another year. Even if I end up out of pocket, Christmas does me good—more good than can ever be measured in money. And so I say: thank God for Christmas!'

Scrooge's clerk, sweltering in his windowless back room, was so carried away by this little speech that he leapt to his feet and began to applaud. Suddenly realising what he'd done, he sat down again in a hurry and picked up his pen, which he then dropped three or four times because both his fingers and the pen were wet with sweat.

Scrooge glared at his one and only employee. 'Don't be such a goose!' he growled. 'One more sound out of you and you'll be searching through the "Positions Vacant"—and there ain't too many positions vacant in Dandaloo Shire, I can tell you that for nothing!'

He spun around on his office chair and faced his nephew once more. He was silent for a while, and then said with sly smile, 'You're not a bad public speaker, young fellah. Ever thought of going into politics? I have one or two contacts—blokes I've done business with in the past. If we could get you into the House of Representatives you could do yourself a bit of good ... and me too. I'm sure you'd be in a position to put a bit of business my way.'

Seeing the look of blank disappointment on his nephew's face, Scrooge snapped, 'All right then, buzz off! Go on, clear out. You've wasted enough of my time. Time's money and I've got work to do.'

'Don't be angry, Uncle Ted. Come and have Christmas dinner with us tomorrow. Go on—come and see us tomorrow.'

'I'll see you dead first!'

'But why?' cried Scrooge's nephew. 'Why?'

Leaning back in his chair Scrooge asked, in a voice that was little more than a murmur, 'Why did you get married?'

'Because I fell in love!'

'Crikey! What a galah!' hooted Scrooge. 'Because you fell in love!' He shook his shaggy old head as if astonished by his nephew's stupidity. 'Good afternoon, and there's the door!'

'Now you know that's not the reason, Uncle Ted. Don't go blaming my wife. You never came to visit me *before* I was married, so it's hardly an excuse for not coming to see me now.'

'In case you didn't hear, I said: "Good afternoon!"'

'I'm not after anything. I haven't got my hand out. I don't want a dollar of your money. But I'm the only living relative you've got left in the world. So why can't we be mates?'

Scrooge lowered his gaze to the contract on his desk and began to read it. Without looking up again he said, 'Good afternoon!'

'Ah well, I've tried. That's all I can do. I guess you can't melt granite. But in the spirit of Christmas, and family, and forgiveness, I've tried. So Merry Christmas, Uncle Ted.'

'Good afternoon!' said Scrooge.

'And a Happy New Year.'

'Good afternoon!' said Scrooge.

His nephew turned and left the small office, carefully closing the front door behind him to keep out the hot wind and the swirling dust. But on the way he paused to say 'Merry Christmas' to the clerk, who responded with his own warm and friendly 'Merry Christmas' in reply.

'Another mug,' muttered Scrooge. 'Two Christmas idiots burbling their meaningless idiocies to each other. It's almost more than a sane man can stand.'

Seeing his clerk staring at him, Scrooge grumbled, 'I know what your salary is. And I know you've got a wife and kids and a mortgage. And if you think you can afford a merry Christmas on your income, then you're a sheep short in the top paddock.'

Pleased with this, Scrooge went back to reading the document on his desk and punching numbers into a small calculator that sat near his right hand. A gust of hot air almost blew the papers onto the floor, and Scrooge looked up to see a young man in a Salvation Army uniform entering the office and closing the door.

'G'day,' said the young man cheerfully. He was the new Salvation Army officer in the Dandaloo district, and he hadn't met Scrooge before—or heard of his reputation.

'Do I have the pleasure of addressing Mr Scrooge or Mr Marley?' he asked pleasantly.

'Marley's dead,' growled Scrooge with an expression on his face as if he'd just eaten a particularly sour lemon. 'Marley died exactly seven years ago today.'

'Sorry to hear that,' said the young Salvation Army officer cheerfully. 'I have no doubt that Mr Marley's generosity is well represented by his surviving partner.'

This statement hit the nail exactly on the head, for Jack Marley and Ted Scrooge were like twins when it came to being tight-fisted. At the sound of the word 'generosity', Scrooge frowned and looked suspiciously at the newcomer.

'At this Christmas season,' said the young Salvation Army captain, pulling out a receipt book, 'we need to think about the less-well-off members of our community—the elderly, the lonely, the ill, the unemployed, the single mums struggling with too many kids and too little money. A bunch of us are organising Christmas hampers for the needy so the kids won't miss out on Christmas presents and the oldies won't feel forgotten, and so they can do what the rest of us do on Christmas Day—have a bang up Christmas dinner.'

'I won't be wasting money on ham or turkey or Christmas pudding,' muttered Scrooge, but he muttered these words to himself so the man in the Salvation Army uniform didn't hear them.

'The spirit of Christmas tells us to reach out and give a helping hand to those less fortunate than ourselves,' the young officer said.

'Has the government stopped paying benefits then?' snarled Scrooge.

'No, no, the government still provides welfare payments.'

'And these "needy" you're yapping about—they can manage to eat on those welfare payments?'

'They get by, of course. But they certainly can't provide anything special for Christmas Day.'

'Good, good,' said Scrooge sarcastically. 'For a moment I thought the government had given up on its job of caring for the poor.'

'The needy are not just the government's responsibility. They're everyone's responsibility.'

'And I exercise my responsibility by paying

outrageously high taxes. It's my tax dollars that are already pouring into the stomachs, and the pockets, of these benefit bludgers. How many welfare cheats are there, then? Answer me that.'

'Some. And government departments do their best to weed them out. Meanwhile, the genuinely poor are with us—and they feel their needs especially at Christmas time, when everyone else has more than enough and can provide nothing special for their children. The old, the ill and the lonely feel especially cut off from the rest of the community at this time of year. If we can provide a Christmas hamper for each of them it will give them more than just material provisions—it will remind them they're not forgotten, not discarded at this Christmas season. That's the spirit of Christian charity. Now, what can I put you down for Mr Scrooge?'

'Nothing!'

'You wish to be anonymous?'

'I wish to be left alone,' Scrooge replied. 'That's what I wish. And that's the only Christmas wish I have. I won't be indulging in such stupidities as presents and cards and expensive food this Christmas, and I can't afford to look after the welfare cheats and benefit bludgers. If they want Christmas hampers, let the government use some of the tax dollars they squeeze out of me to provide them.'

'At Christmas time, Mr Scrooge, these folk need more than bureaucratic handouts. They need to feel that their community hasn't forgotten them.'

'And I haven't forgotten that my business is doing business. I don't interfere in other people's business and I expect them not to interfere in mine. Good afternoon!'

The young Salvation Army officer got the message. He smiled a slight, embarrassed smile at Scrooge, and at the clerk, and hurriedly left the office.

Scrooge resumed reading through the contract before him, and even chuckled quietly, feeling quite pleased with himself.

Meanwhile, the hot wind increased and the red dust thickened so that people ran across the street from one building to another with their heads bent into the breeze and their hands over their mouths to avoid swallowing the choking grit. The Volunteer Bush Fire Brigade building, diagonally opposite Scrooge's office, kept disappearing behind walls of whirling dust. Gusts of blistering wind rattled the windows and doors, and the street was almost deserted. The handful of customers in the Dandaloo Pub settled down to the serious business of drinking their beers and rum chasers, and not shifting an inch until the dust storm finally blew itself out.

Two small boys came whizzing down the street in a billy cart they'd rigged up with a makeshift sail. They yelled steering instructions to each other as blasts of wind drove them along. They collided with a power pole, tumbled out of their overturned billy cart, then leapt up laughing and set off again.

Behind the shop windows, faces could be seen staring out into the street. And every face seemed to say, 'I'm glad I'm indoors and not outside in that!' The owners of those relieved faces laughed and told each other tall tales about other dust storms they'd seen that were much worse than this one. And many of those shop windows were decorated with pieces of Christmas bush, and the shop counters were piled high with Christmas goodies.

Slowly the wind died down, and the dust settled, and the people wandered back out to look at how much of it had been deposited on their cars. They slapped each other on the back and swore that they'd let nothing take the fun out of Christmas, and then they offered to buy each other a beer: 'Just to get the dust outta ya throat.' Soon the Dandaloo Pub was doing a roaring trade, with the blokes washing away the dust, while their wives and kids staggered out to their cars carrying armloads of Christmas presents and Christmas food.

A group of four children from the Dandaloo Primary School—two boys and two girls—set themselves up on a street corner and began singing Christmas carols. One of them held out his cap and collected money from the occasional passer-by. But seeing there was so little pedestrian traffic in that small town, they began walking down the street, stopping at each shop to sing for a while. And at each one the shopkeeper or a customer would come out and drop a few coins in the cap.

When they came to the front window of *Scrooge and Marley—Stock and Station Agents* they began to sing:

Joy to the world,
The Lord has come.
Let earth receive her king.
Let every heart prepare him room,
And heaven and nature sing . . .

At which point they stopped abruptly as they saw Scrooge rise from his desk with a heavy wooden ruler in his hand and an angry scowl on his face. They hurried on to the next shop.

Finally the time came to shut up the office for the day. The clerk looked at the clock on the wall and rose from his desk in the windowless inner office, looking expectantly at Ted Scrooge.

'Yes, yes, all right,' growled Scrooge, 'it's knock off time.'

The clerk hurriedly packed up the things on his desk and took a few steps towards the front door.

'I suppose you'll want to take the whole of tomorrow off, then?' grumbled Scrooge. 'And the day after too?'

'Well … yes … of course … if you don't mind, Mr Scrooge.'

'Mind? Of course I mind! But I'm stuck, aren't I? The whole world goes mad at this time of the year, so I've got no choice. And if I docked you a couple of day's pay you'd whinge about it, I suppose.'

A look of panic passed over the clerk's face for a moment, and then he decided that Scrooge was joking and smiled faintly.

'But I'm the one who's being diddled,' said Scrooge, 'done out of a couple of day's pay with no work in return. Whaddaya say to that?'

'It's only for Christmas Day and Boxing Day—'

'That's a lousy excuse for picking my pocket—just because it's December.'

Scrooge turned to pack away the contracts on his desk in a tall filing cabinet, and the clerk hurried out of the front door while he had the chance. He bustled down the street, around the corner and towards the southern end of town, where his small house stood and his wife and kids were waiting for him. In fact, once he was out of that office his heart became lighter, and he almost ran, shouting 'Merry Christmas' to anyone he passed.

Back in the office Scrooge settled down to read a newspaper that a client had left behind earlier in the day. He enjoyed it all the more knowing it was free. The gloom of twilight had begun to settle by the time he turned off the light and locked the office door. With shuffling steps and the newspaper tucked under his arm, Ted Scrooge made his way home.

He could have lived in the best house, the biggest house, the newest house in all of Dandaloo. But spending money on a new house, Scrooge thought, would be a criminal waste. So he still lived in the cottage that had once belonged to his grandfather. It was a small weatherboard cottage with a corrugated iron roof. It was now quite old—and showing its age. The paint was peeling off the weatherboards because Scrooge couldn't bring himself to spend money on the place. The last blood-red rays of sunset were in the western sky, and long, black shadows filled the street as Scrooge reached his gate.

The front door of Scrooge's cottage faced east, so the door, along with the whole of his small front yard, was sunk in a dim, purple twilight when he mounted the three steps to his verandah and reached out for the door knob.

Now, there was nothing very special about that door knob. I suppose you might have called it very large—door knobs *were* large when Scrooge's grandfather was a young man building the cottage. The knob was made of brass, and it had the sort of well-worn shine about it that only many years and many hands can give.

Furthermore, it must be said that Ted Scrooge had less imagination than any other bloke in Dandaloo. He had less imagination than the president of Dandaloo Shire Council—and that's saying a lot. He even had less imagination than the local Member of Parliament—and that's saying even more! On top of which, in the seven years since Jack Marley had tumbled off the twig, Ted Scrooge had not given his former partner one moment's thought. Not for one single tick of the clock had he thought about old Marley.

In the light of all that, can you explain how it happened that when Scrooge bent over to put his key in the lock, what he saw reflected in his shiny front door knob was not his own face, but the face of Jack Marley?

Marley's face! Quite definitely Jack Marley's face. Not a dim, purple shadow like everything else on that front verandah or in that front yard. No, not dim and purple at all, but glowing, with a pale, unhealthy light. It was Marley's face: every grizzled line of it, with its faint halo of untidy grey hair and its rimless glasses pushed up on its forehead. The hair was moving slightly, as if stirred by a breeze from ... who knows where. The eyes were wide open, and utterly without expression. The flesh had a livid, deathly colour and the mouth was slightly open as if trying to speak. There was something horrible about it, but the horror was not in the face itself—it was more in the expression that said the face was looking at something horrible.

On that baking hot December night, an icy finger ran down Scrooge's spine and he shivered. Then he looked again and saw nothing but a door knob. The same old door knob he had been looking at for years.

He'd pulled his hand back when he'd seen Marley's face. Now he reached hesitantly forward and grasped the key again. He twisted it, producing a solid click in the lock. Then, steeling his nerves, he grabbed the knob, turned it and stepped through the doorway.

Inside was the narrow hallway that ran through the middle of the old-fashioned house. Just an empty hallway, nothing more. Scrooge reached out and flicked on the large, antiquated light switch. A 25-watt light bulb, hanging from a cord in the middle of the hallway, cast its dim, yellow light over all. All the light bulbs in Scrooge's house were 25 watts. It saved money on the electricity bill.

He looked up and down that poorly lit hallway, then to left and right, before he shook himself as if waking from a bad dream. Nothing was there but the same old house he had known all his life. There was the flowered wallpaper his grandmother had chosen many years ago, now so badly faded that it looked like nothing more than pale, brown blotches. The door on his left opened into his bedroom, with its old brass bedstead. On the right was the front parlour, with its ancient, over-stuffed furniture—a room he never used.

'Oh, pooh!' snorted Scrooge. Then as if to give himself confidence, he said again, 'Pooh!'

He turned and slammed the front door behind him. The sound echoed around the small house. Every room seemed to have its own hollow echo. But Scrooge was not a man to be frightened by echoes. Remembering that he had left the key on the outside of the lock, he re-opened the front door, removed the key and closed the door again. Then he locked it from the inside and slid home the heavy bolt that made it doubly secure. Many people in that small outback town never bothered to lock their houses, but Scrooge trusted nobody.

He walked slowly around that small cottage and did something he'd never done before—he turned on every light in the house. He looked into the front parlour, and his own bedroom, and the large country kitchen, the small laundry, the bathroom, the back room, and the spare bedroom that he used as a store room. Every room looked just as it should. Nothing was out of place. He opened up his big old-fashioned wardrobe and looked inside. He even looked under his bed. Nobody was there, nothing was out of place.

Scrooge heaved a loud sigh and began to breathe more easily. Realising how foolish he'd been, he walked around the house again and turned off all the lights, except the one yellow bulb in the kitchen. He took the newspaper from under his arm and put it on the solid old kitchen table. Nothing could be heard in that dark house except the loud, slow ticking of the long-case clock that had once belonged to Scrooge's grandfather and that now stood in the back room.

The house was hot and airless, so Scrooge pushed open the kitchen window and opened a window in the back room, hoping to get some slight movement of air between the two. Then he saw a scribbled note lying in the middle of the kitchen table. He picked it up and squinted at it in the dim light. It had been written by Mrs O'Riley, who came and cleaned for him one day a week.

'I made a salad for you,' it said, 'and put it in the fridge. It's only a small salad 'coz I couldn't find much food in the house.'

Then, as an afterthought, she had written underneath, 'Merry Christmas'.

Scrooge sank down into one of the straight-backed kitchen chairs and let the note drop from his fingers onto the floor. For some reason he didn't feel like eating even a small salad. In fact, he didn't feel like eating anything.

Facing Scrooge where he sat was an old kitchen dresser, and in the middle of that dresser was a row of tea cups hanging by their handles from wooden pegs. As he watched those tea cups, they began to quiver and tremble. First just one at the end of the row, then another, and another, and then all of them. They trembled so fiercely that they rattled and clinked. Scrooge feared they might start leaping off their wooden pegs and throwing themselves onto the floor.

The clinking and rattling went on for half a minute, or perhaps a minute, but to Scrooge it felt like an hour. Then, just as suddenly as it had started, it stopped—and the cottage was silent again. In fact, somehow it felt more silent than before.

To break the silence Scrooge said loudly, 'Humbug! Tommyrot! Nonsense!' He stood up abruptly, but feeling slightly unsteady on his feet sat down again. He snorted loudly.

Then he heard the footsteps. They were slow, heavy footsteps ... the footsteps of someone who was diseased or old—or dead. 'Humbug!' snapped Scrooge again, but rather more quietly this time. And there was another sound as well, a metallic sound, a clanking sound, as if those footsteps were dragging a heavy chain behind them.

'It's humbug!' said Scrooge for the third time. 'I refuse to believe it. It must be kids playing jokes on me. None of 'em like me.' Nevertheless, he had gone quite pale. Even in that faint, yellow light his face looked white. And the footsteps were getting louder, and closer. They seemed to be coming down the hallway from the direction of the front door—the locked and bolted front door.

With a sudden movement, Scrooge leapt up and pushed the kitchen door closed. Then he dragged his chair to the opposite side of the kitchen, as far away as he could get, and sat down again, his eyes glued on the door. He watched the knob, waiting for it to turn. But it didn't turn. The sound reached the other side of the door and kept on coming, without turning the knob, without opening the door. As it came through the solid wooden door, the sickly yellow light bulb seemed to flicker and flare, as if to say, 'I recognise him! I know him! It's Marley's Ghost!' And then it dimmed once more.

It was definitely him: the same face, the same worn boots he refused to get repaired, the same old grey trousers, the same faded business shirt with the frayed cuffs and collar, the same wispy grey hair, the same cold, meaningless expression that so many creditors had come to dread. Wound around his middle was a heavy chain that dragged on the floor behind him like some sinister steel snake. Bound up in the chain were account books, and petty cash boxes, and calculators, and wallets, and contracts, and invoices, and bills. The body was transparent so that Scrooge could see straight through it to the door beyond—which was still firmly closed.

Scrooge had often heard it said that Marley had no heart, and now he had every reason to believe it was true.

Not that he really believed it even now. For Scrooge didn't want to believe that what he was seeing was real. Even as he felt those dead-cold eyes fall on him, Scrooge still fought against the evidence of his senses and told himself that this wasn't really happening.

The night was still, hot and airless, but the silence that stood between those two figures was as cold as the grave.

At last Scrooge spluttered, 'Whaddaya want?'

In a droning, lifeless voice Marley replied, 'Much!' And Scrooge shivered, for it was Marley's voice, no doubt about it.

'Much!' it said again.

'Who are you?' asked Scrooge, although he knew the answer.

'Ask me, rather, who I *was*,' replied the Phantom.

'Don't be so picky,' snapped Scrooge. 'I didn't know ghosts were so pedantic. All right then, who *were* you?'

'In life I was your partner, Jack Marley.'

'Can you . . . can you . . . sit down?' Scrooge asked hesitantly.

'I can.'

'Okay then, sit down. So I don't have to keep looking up at you.'

Scrooge had asked the question because he wasn't if a spectre so transparent could sit on a chair without floating right through it. He hadn't wanted to just order it to sit—it might have been embarrassing if the Spirit had ended up on the floor.

The thing that had once been Marley gestured with its hand. One of the wooden straight-backed chairs slid out from the kitchen table and the Spectre sat down on it.

'You don't believe in me,' said the apparition.

'No, I don't,' snorted Scrooge emphatically. 'I had a roast beef sandwich for lunch that I bought at the pub. The meat must have been off.'

'So you doubt your own senses then?'

'Or the gravy. There was gravy on the roast beef sandwich and I'll bet it was days old and full of strange bacteria. That's what's doing this to me— bacteria. Yes, that's where you come from: the gravy . . . not the grave.'

Ted Scrooge chuckled because he quite liked his little joke, and since he very rarely made jokes, he enjoyed it while he could. Besides, it kept the butter-flies in his stomach from fluttering too much, and stopped his fingers from trembling nervously, and generally prevented the terrors from overtaking him and making him scream out loud.

But now the hairs on the back of Scrooge's neck were rising under the dead-cold gaze of the Ghost's eyes. The Ghost itself sat perfectly still, not moving, not blinking, not breathing. Well, obviously not breathing—it had given up the need to do that seven years earlier.

A sweat broke out on Scrooge's forehead, and it wasn't caused by the hot, still night. To distract himself from the wave of terror that threatened to engulf him, Scrooge picked up an old toothpick that was lying on the table.

'See this toothpick?' Scrooge asked the Ghost.

'I see it.'

'You're not looking at it, you're looking at me.'

'But still I see it.'

'Well then, all I have to do is chew on this old toothpick and swallow it, and before long I'll be haunted by pains and apparitions and ghosts and ghouls—all of my own making. So there's no reason why I should believe in you. You're a delirium from a bad sandwich, not a spectre from beyond the grave. Humbug!'

At this the Spirit threw back its head and issued a frightful, dismal howl—a howl that would wake the dead to hear. Not that the dead needed waking, for the dead already sat at Scrooge's kitchen table. As the apparition howled, its chains clanked and rattled in a horribly threatening fashion. Then the Spirit glared at Scrooge with a terrible stare that seemed to slice open his very soul.

At this Scrooge slid off his chair, dropped to his knees and covered his face with his hands.

'Don't, don't,' he whispered. 'Whatever you are, and wherever you come from, why are you doing this to me?'

'You sad, narrow-minded old man,' replied the Ghost. 'So you believe in me or not?'

'Yes,' whimpered Scrooge, 'I do. I must. I can't avoid it now. But why? Why does a spectre like you walk the earth on this Christmas Eve? And why do you come to me?'

'It is required of every man that he serve his fellow creatures,' the Ghost responded. 'Each one of us is required to love God with all our heart, all our mind, all our soul and all our strength, and to love our neighbours just as much as we love ourselves.

And if we refuse to do so in our lifetime, then we are doomed to wander forever, in lonely death, cut off from those we failed to love. No one sees us. No one hears us. We remain utterly alone, staring forever into our own black, selfish, empty hearts. But this one Christmas Eve I have been given the chance to come to the one man on earth who could see my face and hear my voice—for his heart is already as black and cold as mine. So I come to you as a lonely, wandering witness, to serve you in death as I never served you life. You were my neighbour, sitting just a desk away from me. But I never gave you a word of kindness, encouragement, advice or help!'

At this the shadowy figure again let out a crying sob, and its chain trembled in its ghostly hands.

'Why the chains?' said Scrooge, trembling. 'Explain the chains to me.'

'I wear the chain I forged in life,' said the disembodied soul. 'I made it link by link. I wound it about myself so tightly that I cannot now remove it. Would you like to know the weight and length of the chain that you are weaving around yourself, day by day? It was as long as this, and as heavy as this, seven years ago. And you have kept on working on it ever since. Tonight it is as cumbersome as a deep sea anchor chain.'

Scrooge looked down at the floor, expecting to see the heavy iron chain already there, coiled around his feet.

'Jack!' he pleaded. 'Old Jack Marley, my old partner! Tell me more! Say something that will help me!'

'I have no help or comfort to give,' the Ghost replied. 'That must come from others. And my time with you is almost gone. I am restless, always restless, and I cannot stay much longer. I cannot settle any-where. In my life I stuck to my narrow groove—our office, my house, the pub for a drink after work, the football club on Saturday night. It was a very small, very narrow circle. Now my circle is wide and I must keep endlessly, restlessly drifting. It is a weary, empty, lonely journey that I now face.'

It was a habit with Scrooge that whenever he had to think he would thrust his hands into his pockets. His clients used to say he did it so that no one else could get their hands on his money. He did it now as he thought about what the spirit of Jack Marley said.

'So, seven years you've been doing this wandering business,' said Scrooge. 'You've been out on your ghostly wallaby track like some phantom swagman for that long and you still haven't found a homestead?'

'There is nowhere to find. There is no company, no community, no family, no habitation—I rejected all of that when I rejected our loving Maker and Ruler who bids us care for each other. And so I wander. No rest. No peace. Just endless, bitter, angry remorse.'

'Angry? Who are you angry with?'

'Sometimes with myself. Sometimes with others who let me sink into selfishness and didn't stop me. Sometimes with the whole, wide world.'

'This wandering you're yabbering on about—do you travel fast?'

'On the wings of the wind,' replied the Ghost.

'Well, you should have covered a bit of territory in seven years, then.'

These words triggered another plaintive howl from the apparition, the hideous noise echoing through the dead silence of that sweltering house. In fact, Scrooge half expected the local police constable to start knocking on his front door with a noise pollution complaint.

'Oh, oh,' it sobbed, 'I'm a captive, bound in loneliness. The people of this planet know so little of what awaits. They don't know how best to use the short span that stretches from the cradle to the grave. They don't know the vast, empty aeons of regret that lie before me, and all those like me!'

Starting to think of himself, Scrooge began to look around for some defence or justification. 'But you were always a good businessman, Jack,' he faltered.

'Business!' cried the Ghost, and the word became another howl. 'My business should have been care for my neighbours. My true business was concern and charity; my business was faith, hope and love. Of course, I was sometimes thoughtful, sometimes charitable—but instead of an ocean of concern I offered an eyedropper.'

The Spectre raised the chains on its phantom arms, then flung them heavily, despairingly onto the floor again.

'At this time of the year I suffer most,' the Spirit sobbed. 'When the spirit of Christmas, of fellowship, of good will walks the streets, it is then I am most alone. It's as if I spent my life with my eyes cast down at the dirt, never once looking up to the Star that led the Wise Men from the East to the cradle in which our hope was born.'

Scrooge became alarmed at the sheer misery of the presence before him, and his fingers began to twitch nervously.

'Listen to me!' cried the Ghost. 'My time is nearly gone.'

'I'm listening, I'm listening! Just get to the point and don't waste words.'

'How it happens that I have come to appear before you in a shape that you recognise, I don't know. I've often sat beside you in our old office, unseen and unheard—an invisible presence at your elbow.'

The idea that a Ghost had often shared the office was not a pleasant one, and Scrooge shivered slightly.

'I'm here tonight,' the apparition went on, 'to warn you that you still have a chance to escape my terrible fate.'

'Well, that's good news, at least,' said Scrooge. 'You always were a mate to me, Jack Marley.'

'You will be haunted,' continued the Ghost, 'by Three Spirits.'

Scrooge's face fell. 'And that's supposed to be good news? Are you off your rocker? Has death finally driven you bonkers? How can being haunted be good news? Is this the chance you spoke of?'

'It is.'

'In that case, I think I just might give it a miss. Why don't you pop off like a good bloke and haunt someone else instead?'

'Without their visits,' said the Ghost, 'you cannot hope to avoid the awful path I now tread. Expect the first to arrive at one o'clock in the morning—just as the town hall bell strikes.'

'How about sending them all at once, in a mob, and getting it over and done with?'

'The second will arrive on the next night at the

same time. The third on the next night, just as the town hall clock is striking midnight. Now I go, and you'll see me no more. But remember all of this, Ted Scrooge. Don't forget a word!'

With this the Ghost rose from the kitchen chair and flung its chain over its arm. It walked slowly around the kitchen towards the open window. It beckoned Scrooge to step a little closer, which he did. When he was two paces away, Marley's Spirit held up its hand for him to stop.

At that gesture by the Ghost, a chorus of voices reached Scrooge's ears—wailing, crying, miserable voices. Each voice could be heard accusing itself, and then trying to justify itself, and then accusing itself once more. It was a mournful, anguished sound. Marley's Ghost opened its mouth and joined the dismal choir. As it did so it dissolved into a curling wisp of smoke and drifted out of the open window. Filled with curiosity, Scrooge went and looked out.

The window looked over an empty block of land with a large gum tree in the middle. Round and round that gum tree a countless mob of phantoms circled through the air. They moved restlessly, urgently, all moaning as they went, and all bearing heavy chains. A few of them Scrooge recognised as men he'd known during their earthly lives: one had been a banker, another a politician, and yet another a lawyer with whom Scrooge had often had dealings in years gone by.

Then the hot wind sprang up again, and with it came the dry, gritty dust. Soon clouds of the stuff had either obscured the spirits or driven them away. Scrooge closed the window to keep the dust out and then went to check the front door through which the Ghost had entered.

He found it as he had left it: locked and bolted.

Scrooge turned off the kitchen light and walked down the hallway to his bedroom, feeling weary and light-headed. Without taking off his clothes, he flopped onto the mattress, and whether from the heat of the day or from nervous exhaustion, he fell asleep in less than a minute.

The Second Verse: The Ghost of Christmas Past

Scrooge woke up suddenly and found that it was still dark—pitch black, in fact. He lay in bed, slowly coming to his senses and trying to pierce the total blackness and make out the dim outline of the window, or his wardrobe, or ... anything.

Just then the clock in the Dandaloo Town Hall clock tower began to chime.

Scrooge closed his eyes and counted the chimes. To his astonishment they kept on ringing out—nine, ten, eleven, twelve. No! snorted Scrooge. He had looked at the kitchen clock when he went to bed, and it was two o'clock in the morning then. For it to be pitch black and chiming twelve he must have slept through a whole day and a night. Impossible!

'It was that dust,' said Scrooge, 'that's what it was. That fine, red, gritty dust must have got into the works of the town hall clock and bunged up the striking mechanism. Either that, or it's twelve midday.'

That was an alarming thought—if it was midday,

then he'd been struck blind! He stumbled out of bed, groped his way to the bedroom window and flung open the curtains. Although there was no moon, he could make out faint starlight through the branches of the gum trees that lined the street. Whatever time it really was, it was still the middle of the night. The temperature had begun to drop, as it does in inland towns, from blazing hot during the day to chilly overnight.

If it was night time, then the problem was definitely the clock chiming the wrong time. He'd write a letter to the shire president about it first thing on Monday!

Scrooge found the discovery that he hadn't lost a complete day reassuring. Many of the contracts locked in the ancient safe back in his office depended on days: 'payment due in 28 days', 'in 14 days', 'in 90 days'. If he could lose days he could lose money: an alarming thought to Scrooge.

Still staring out of the window at the dark, silent street, Scrooge shivered. Not that he was really cold, just a little chilly. The shiver actually came from the memory of Marley's Ghost. As he walked over to his wardrobe and pulled out his old dressing gown, Scrooge turned that event over and over in his mind. By the time he was pulling the dressing gown on over the clothes he still wore, he had convinced himself that it had merely been a dream. Or rather, a nightmare.

'I must have come home and fallen asleep,' Scrooge muttered to himself. 'Maybe I was so tired I nodded off in a kitchen chair. Yes, that was it. And I was so uncomfortable that I had a nightmare.'

But he shivered again at the memory of the

conversation with his dead partner. He sat down on the bed, pulled off his shoes and replaced them with slippers. Then he fell back on top of the bedcovers again as some part of his mind kept asking, 'Was it a nightmare, or not?'

He lay there, unable to fall asleep again, troubled by the fact that he couldn't quite convince himself Marley's Ghost had just been a dream. A full hour passed while he argued the matter over and over in his mind. Then the town hall clock chimed again. This time it chimed only once—just one solemn, heavy 'dong'.

'Stupid clock,' murmured Scrooge, still convinced it was wrong. 'Anyway, if it was right, according to Marley's Ghost, something would have happened by now.'

He lay on his bed listening to the deep, distant sound fade away into the night. 'I didn't come down in the last shower,' he told himself. 'I knew nothing was going to happen.' But just as that booming 'dong' died away to complete silence, something did.

Lights suddenly flashed in Scrooge's room. His eyes flew wide open and he turned his head—and found a ghostly face just inches away from his own!

Attached to that face was a ghostly figure. It stood close beside his bed and bent over Scrooge where he lay. It looked a bit like an unhealthy child and a bit like a shrunken old man. It had long, thin strands of white hair, but its pale, grey face had none of the wrinkles of old age. The ghostly skin was smooth and unmarked. Its arms and legs were long and wiry and muscular—as the arms and legs of country kids are. Its feet were bare, as country kids' feet so often are. But it wasn't a country kid—that ghostly flesh looked as if it had never seen the sunlight. And its eyes weren't the eyes of a kid, but of an old, old man.

It wore a white tunic sort of outfit, as if it was about to play the role of an angel in the Christmas pageant at the local school. Around its waist was a belt with a strange, unearthly, luminous green glow. In its hand was a branch of Christmas bush. But perhaps strangest of all was that out of the top of its head shot a brilliant, laser-like beam of light that lit up the whole room.

As Scrooge stared, wide-eyed, at this Thing, he decided that the light was *not* the strangest thing about it. Its belt sparkled and glittered and gleamed, sometimes brightly and sometimes faintly, and sometimes in one part of the belt and sometimes in another. And as these lights changed the Thing seemed to change with it. Sometimes it glowed pale green, sometimes pale blue and sometimes even pale purple. Sometimes it faded to near invisibility and sometimes it was very clear and distinct.

'Well, starve the lizards!' said Scrooge softly. Then pulling himself together he nervously asked, 'Are you the Spirit whose visit I was warned about?'

'I am!'

Its voice was very soft—little more than a whisper. And although it was only inches from his ear, to Scrooge it sounded as if it came from very far away.

'Who are you?' demanded Scrooge.

'I am the Ghost of Christmas Past.'

'What past? Of history? Of long past?'

'No. Your past.'

Scrooge couldn't have told you why, but he found the light streaming from the Thing's head very disturbing. So he pointed to an old Akubra hat lying on a chair in the corner and asked it to cover its head.

'What?' gasped the Ghost. 'Do you already want to put out the little light that I can give you? It's bad enough that you've spent years trying to turn down the dimmer switch on my light, but now you want to turn it off altogether!'

'No need to get your knickers in a knot. I wasn't having a go at you or anything,' replied Scrooge, puzzled about when he was supposed to have tried to turn down the Ghost's 'dimmer switch'. Unable to think of an answer, he asked, 'All right, why are you here then? Why have you come?'

'To open your eyes.'

'There's nothing wrong with my eyes. For an old bloke my eyes are pretty good.'

'But still you don't see.'

'A decent night's sleep in my bed would be better for my old eyes than you turning up and trying to frighten a bloke out of his wits.'

'You are blind to your future because you can't truly see your own past.'

With these words the Thing reached out its strong right hand and took a firm hold on Scrooge's upper arm.

'Come! I'm taking you for a little stroll.'

There would have been no point in Scrooge complaining that the heat of the day was gone and it was now chilly outside. There would have been no point in saying that he was wearing his slippers and his dressing gown over his day clothes. There would have been no point in protesting that he'd look like a real goose walking around dressed like that. And even less point in saying that he'd much rather go back to bed.

The Spirit pulled Scrooge towards the bedroom window, slid it open and leapt lightly up onto the sill.

'It's a bit of a drop from there,' warned Scrooge. 'It's okay for you, but I'm just flesh and blood—and fairly old flesh and blood at that. I reckon I might fall.'

The Ghost reached over and laid its hand on Scrooge's chest, just above his heart.

'Now,' said the Spirit, 'you shall be as light as air in all our travels together.'

With these words the Thing jumped out of the window and Scrooge found that he was carried with it. They didn't fall. In fact, they didn't land on the ground at all. Instead of falling down from the window sill they fell *upwards*! At least, they rose swiftly into the air. But their journey lasted only a moment.

They were standing on a country road—a rough, dirt road marked with the wheel ruts of many vehicles over many years. Near where they had landed was a farm gate, with a roadside mail box beside it. And beyond the gate, at the end of a long track, was a small farmhouse with a corrugated iron roof and a wide verandah around all four sides. All of this Scrooge could see clearly because although the night had been moonless when he fell asleep, there was now a full moon, and the whole landscape was bathed in a brilliant blue glow.

'Do you recognise this place?' asked the Spirit.

'Stone the crows! My old home! I was born here. I was a boy here.'

The Spirit turned and looked at Scrooge. But the old man was unaware of the Thing's deep, penetrating gaze, for Scrooge was suddenly thinking a thousand thoughts, swept up in a thousand memories. There were smells he could remember: of newly harvested wheat, of the chook yard, of dust carried on a dry summer breeze. There were sounds that came back to him: the bone-rattling clatter of his father's old tractor, the distant sound of sheep and cattle, the much softer sound of the creek in the bottom paddock trickling between the roots of river red gums.

Each smell and sound brought with it a thunder of thoughts. For just a moment he was a boy again, full of hopes and joys and plans and dreams.

'Is that the gleam of a tear I see in your eye?' asked the Ghost.

Scrooge was silent for a moment, then muttered, 'Just a bit of dust. Something got in my eye, that's all. Well, get on with it then. Take me wherever you want to.'

'Do you remember the way?' asked the Spirit.

'Remember it?' cried Scrooge. 'I could walk it blindfold!'

'A bit strange then,' said the Thing beside him, 'that you forgot it so completely for so many years. But let's go on.'

They started along the track, and Scrooge was astonished to notice that they walked right *through* the wooden bars of the farm gate without opening it: both of them, not just the Spirit. He thought this must have something to do with the effect the Ghost was having on him. At the farmhouse he recognised the tree where he'd built a cubby house, the posts of the verandah where he'd chased the possums, the backyard where he'd trained his dog, and the home paddock where he'd kept the old horse he'd ridden as a boy.

Then they were in the air again, covering miles in an instant, and coming to a halt in a small bush town. There was the wooden bridge over the creek, and the railway station, and the pub, and the church spire—just as Scrooge remembered them all. And there was the one-room school building, and in the yard in front of it were jostling, jumping boys and girls leaving school for the start of the holidays. How Scrooge knew that it was the start of the holidays he didn't understand—but he did know. Some of the kids were untying their horses from the peppercorn trees and climbing onto their backs; others were getting their bikes out of the bike shed.

All the time they were shouting and laughing and in high spirits.

'These are but the shadows of times past,' the Ghost explained. 'They cannot see us.'

The crowd of noisy kids split up as they left the school yard. Some went with groups of friends; some rode beside a best mate, shouting plans for the holidays as they went. These were the Christmas holidays that were beginning! That was the cause of all the excitement. The girls were planning Christmas parties and the boys were planning Christmas pranks.

Scrooge couldn't understand why these cheerful young voices were warming his heart and giving him an almost youthful sense of excitement and pleasure. He had no place in his life for excitement and pleasure! He had no place for Christmas holidays!

He was a man of business, and Christmas holidays were a criminal waste of time!

'That school room is not quite empty,' said the Ghost. 'There is one child who has been left alone by his friends. He is still there.'

Scrooge whispered, 'Yes, I know,' and gave one silent sob.

They drifted inside the little yellow-painted weatherboard building that looked like every other one-teacher school in every other outback town. There were rows of desks and hard wooden seats. The air was hot and dry and still, and the room smelled of stale sandwiches. At the front a young man was wiping down a blackboard, and in the middle of the room sat one small boy, looking forlorn and lonely and lost at his desk. His head was down, buried in a storybook.

'I'm sorry your Mum and Dad can't look after you these school holidays,' said the young teacher, turning around from the blackboard. 'But my wife and I are quite happy to put you up in the teacher's house for a few weeks.'

The boy didn't look up. He knew why the teacher and his wife were happy—because they were being paid to provide room and board for him. But he would be the only boy in the house—with the teacher (who had better things to do), and the teacher's wife (who was always complaining of her aches and pains), and their little baby (who cried all the time). All the other kids belonged to a gang or a mob of friends, but he didn't. So they wouldn't be coming out to the teacher's house behind the school to find him and ask him to play with them.

And as the teacher tidied up his desk at the front

of the classroom, old Scrooge sat down on one of the small, hard school chairs and wept to see his poor, forgotten self as he used to be.

While they watched, pictures seemed to form in the air above the boy's head, cloudy at first, then bright and clear and colourful.

'Look! Look!' cried Scrooge, with an enthusiasm no one had heard in his voice for thirty years. 'Look— there's Long John Silver, and Jim Hawkins, and Squire Trelawney, and old Blind Pew! And there's Silver's parrot winging through the air to land on his shoulder! And look there in his hand—the map of the island showing where the treasure is buried.'

As suddenly as it had come, the excitement was gone. In a quiet, subdued voice Scrooge said, 'Books were a better place to be than the real world in those days.' After a pause he added, 'Poor boy.'

Ted Scrooge wiped his eyes on the cuff of his dressing gown as he said, 'I wish ...' But then he stopped, paused and finally said, 'But it's too late now.' He slid his hand into his dressing gown pocket.

'What's the matter?' asked the Ghost.

'Nothing,' said Scrooge. 'Only ... there were some kids singing a Christmas carol in front of my office yesterday afternoon, and I wish I'd given ... ah, well. That's all.'

The Ghost's pale face appeared to smile, then it waved its strong right hand and said in a command-ing voice, 'Let's visit another Christmas!'

As the Spirit waved its hand the room changed. It was the same room, but right in front of their eyes the boy grew taller and older. The school room also looked older, as if it hadn't had a coat of paint in years. The textbooks on the bookshelf out the front looked older and more worn, and there were a few more maps hanging on the walls. The same teacher could be seen through a window walking away from the school building towards the teacher's house. He also looked older and his hair thinner.

Scrooge didn't understand how the change had happened before his eyes; he only knew it had. The boy—the older, taller boy—was no longer sitting at a desk reading. He was now pacing restlessly up and down the small classroom, looking sad and worried and glancing often towards the door.

Then a sound came from the schoolyard, and the boy hurried out onto the verandah. A pony cart, driven by a small girl, came in through the gate into the yard and pulled to a halt. The girl who laid the reins on the pony's back and leapt out of the cart was much younger than the boy.

She ran towards him, threw her arms around him and kissed him. 'My big brother!' she said. 'My wonderful big brother!' And he smiled and laughed and hugged his little sister.

When at last he put her down, she said with a happy grin, 'I've come to bring you home!'

'Home, little Ruthie?' asked the boy, raising one eyebrow.

'Yes!' cried the child, as if she was almost exploding with happiness. 'Home for good and for all. Home for ever and ever.'

'But Dad—'

'Dad's much better. He's different. He's not . . .'

'Not drinking?'

'Not any more! All that has changed! He's quiet now, and kind, and gentle, and so I asked if you could come home, and he said yes, you could. And he sent me in the pony cart to come and fetch you. And he said you should come back and help run the farm and help pay off the debt. And you're to be home in time for Christmas, and it'll be the best Christmas we've ever had!'

'You're quite a girl, little Ruthie,' laughed the boy. Then taking the girl by the hand he hurried around to the teacher's house behind the school, and introduced Ruthie to the teacher (who was polite but uninterested) and the teacher's wife (who barely noticed anyone except her own children). Then, while the boy packed his bags, his sister tried to talk to the teacher's son, who ran around the house like a destructive whirlwind while his distracted mother tried to cope with her new baby (who also never stopped screaming).

At last the boy was packed and had said his farewells, and the two hurried out to the pony cart. Ruthie insisted on taking the reins. 'I love driving old Snowy,' she said as she tapped the pony's back with the leather straps. 'Besides which, he knows me and always does what I say.'

'She was always a delicate creature,' said the Ghost. 'Never strong. She had a lot of illness one way and another. But she had a big heart.'

'Oh, yes!' said Scrooge. 'The biggest, warmest heart that ever was. She was a wonderful sister, was my Ruthie.'

'And even though she died young,' continued the Ghost, 'she married I believe. And had children.'

'One child. A boy.'

'Ah, yes,' said the Ghost, 'your nephew.'

There was a long, heavy silence before Scrooge muttered, 'Yes.'

Then the school yard was gone, just as the pony trap was disappearing down the road, and the road was no longer an empty, dusty country road, but a busy city street filled with honking cars, the old fashioned cars of yesterday, and hurrying pedestrians and hustle everywhere. Here too it was Christmas— decorations hung in the shop windows, and one brightly lit window in a department store showed a Nativity Scene.

The Ghost kept gliding down the street towards the harbour until he came to a warehouse, and above the warehouse floor were the brightly lit windows of the office. Here the Ghost stopped and asked Scrooge if he knew it.

'Of course I know it!' said Scrooge. 'This is where I learned the trade. This is where I learned how to do business.'

They drifted silently in through the door. Inside was a rather old-fashioned office, full of mechanical typewriters and calculating machines and large ledger books. One corner was divided off by a glass partition, and seated at the desk behind it was an overweight, red-faced man who was running his pencil up and down columns of figures.

'It's Maginnis!' cried old Scrooge with excitement. 'It's Maginnis alive again! Ah, he was a good boss.'

Old Maginnis put down his pencil, glanced at the clock, straightened his tie and chuckled to himself. Then he called out in his comfortable, fat, jolly voice:

'Hey, you blokes! Ted! Sid!'

Scrooge's former self was now a young man, and he walked into the glass-partitioned office accompanied by another trainee accountant.

Old Scrooge turned to the Ghost and said, 'Sid Baker! That's who it is. Couldn't mistake him. We were great mates, Sid and me, we really were.'

Maginnis clapped his fat hands together and cried, 'That's it! No more work tonight—it's Christmas Eve. Pack everything up—ledgers and cash box in the safe, everything else in the files so we'll know where to find things when we sober up on New Year's Day.' And the old man laughed at his own joke. 'Get going, Ted! Hop to it, Sid!'

The two young men set about the task of packing up the office work so swiftly and energetically that within minutes it was all done. Meanwhile, Maginnis had looked out of the window and seen a car arriving, so he hurried downstairs and opened the warehouse door so the car and its occupants could enter. Just as Ted and Sid completed their task of packing away, they heard the sound of a party of people trooping up the stairs from the warehouse below.

In through the office door came Maginnis, and Mrs Maginnis, and the three Maginnis daughters. They were carrying a Christmas cake and a hamper full of good things. One of the daughters was carrying a small portable record player. She found a power point and plugged the player in, and soon the sound of Christmas music was filling the room.

Before long they were joined by some young friends of the Maginnis daughters, and the caretaker from downstairs also came up for the party. A couple of the new arrivals pushed the desks back against the walls so they could dance, and soon everyone was kicking up their heels—even old Maginnis and Mrs Maginnis.

Out of a crate came cold cans of beer for the hot dancers, and Mrs Maginnis even produced a chilled bottle of champagne—like a magician pulling a rabbit out of a hat. From a box under Maginnis's desk (which no one knew he'd hidden there) came a large supply of Christmas crackers, and soon everyone was pulling crackers, and reading out corny jokes, and wearing silly paper hats. And when they needed refreshment there were slices of cold turkey and ham, and the Christmas cake was cut up and handed around.

Then from somewhere else in the hamper the youngest Miss Maginnis produced a supply of mince pies, and shortbread biscuits, and a box of chocolates. Refreshed and refuelled, the dancers began again, dancing more energetically than artistically around the room, and occasionally colliding with pieces of office furniture to loud shrieks of laughter.

And old Maginnis seemed to dance more than anyone else, and make more bad jokes than anyone else, and generally work himself into a lather to make sure that everyone else had a good time. When the clock struck eleven, Mrs Maginnis announced that it was time the party broke up so that they could take their daughters to church at midnight.

Mr and Mrs Maginnis lined up at the office door and shook hands with everyone as they left, wishing each and every one of them a Merry Christmas.

'Such a simple matter,' said the Ghost, 'and such a small matter to make these people so cheerful and so full of gratitude.'

'Small?' echoed Scrooge.

'He has spent but a small amount of his own money,' said the Ghost, 'and yet everyone is delighted with the party and everyone is saying what a fine fellow old Maginnis is.'

'No, no,' disagreed Scrooge, 'it's not how much he spends. It's what he does, and what he says. It's his way of entering into the spirit of the thing. It's his words, his looks, his jokes, his laughter. It's just everything he does. And it's the way he does it. It's the very fact that he thought to organise such a simple, joyful event at all. It's the fact that he and his wife gave some thought to planning and preparing it—the very fact that they took a little effort to make others happy.'

As he said these words Scrooge felt the Spirit's gaze fixed firmly upon him, and he stopped.

'What!' said Scrooge. 'What is it?'

'Is something the matter?' asked the Ghost.

'Nothing in particular,' said Scrooge.

'Something rather than nothing, I think,' responded the Ghost.

'No, not at all. No. It's just that ... I'd like to be able to say a word or two to my clerk just at the moment, that's all.'

'My time grows short,' observed the Spirit. 'Quick!'

The result of these words was immediate. Once again Scrooge saw himself. He was older now—a man in the prime of life. His face did not yet have about it the wrinkled, squinting, shrivelled-up look it was to have in old age. Nevertheless, there was something about his appearance that was already unattractive. The eyes were too keen, the eyelids half closed, the glint too eager for profit. Although the face was still unmarked, the eyes spoke of greed—and of nothing but greed.

He was not alone but sat by the side of an attractive, fair-haired young woman. She was wearing dark clothes, and tears glistened in her eyes as she continued to mourn her father. But he was also the one who had opposed her marriage to Ted Scrooge, and now nothing stood in the way of the couple who sat together on a sofa in the front parlour of a sheep station on the outskirts of Dandaloo.

'Be honest with me, Ted,' she was saying. 'I no longer occupy your heart as I once did.'

'What do you mean?'

'Your heart has been given to another.'

'There's no other girl, Beth. I don't know how you can think that.'

'That's not what I think, Ted. I don't think I've lost to someone younger or prettier—I think I lost your heart to something I can't compete with.'

'What do you mean?'

'You know what I mean, Ted. Money takes first place in your life now, and in your heart. There's no room for me.'

'Huh!' snorted the younger Scrooge. 'That's the way the world thinks. The world despises nothing so much as poverty. At the same time the world looks down its nose at those who work hard at making wealth. And the world pretends to despise the rich. Look at any movie you like—the rich men are always the villains. But even so, everyone wants what money can provide. Everyone buys lottery tickets. And everyone in a position of authority is polite and considerate towards the very rich. They despise the means of making wealth, but grovel towards the ones who have it. You're just as muddled about money as the wide world is.'

'And you, Ted, think too much about what the world thinks. You're too desperate, too hungry, too grasping to see what you're doing.'

'Those are harsh words, Beth.'

'Maybe I say them hoping your eyes will open to what you've become, and you'll change.'

'I'm doing better than ever. I don't need to change.'

'That's what I was afraid of,' said the young woman sadly. 'I've seen all those characteristics that were best about you fall away, one by one, until all that is left is your master driving passion.'

'Well, if I've grown wiser as I've grown older, so what? I haven't changed towards you.'

She shook her head slowly and the tears glistened again in her eyes.

'So, you're saying I've changed towards you too—is that it?'

'Our engagement has been a long one, Ted. It was made when we were both poor—when my father was struggling with hard seasons and low wool prices and a big debt at the bank. All we wanted in those days was each other. We didn't care about money.'

'And we would have married then if your father hadn't stood in the way, and if you hadn't decided that you wouldn't marry without his blessing.'

'Perhaps he saw in you, even then, something that I'm seeing only now.'

'But all through this long engagement I've stayed faithful,' protested the younger Scrooge. 'I've never asked you to release me from my commitment, have I?'

'Not in words you haven't, no. Never.'

'Well then?'

'In a changed nature, in a changed ambition in life, in a whole different way of thinking about what matters in life—that's how you've rejected me. Tell me, Ted,' said the girl, looking at him gently, 'if this engagement didn't already exist, would you have sought me out? Would you have tried to win me now? Would you have proposed now?'

It seemed he couldn't deny the honesty of those words, yet he couldn't quite bring himself to admit them either. He swallowed hard and said with a struggle, 'So that's what you think, is it?'

'I wish I thought otherwise,' she answered. 'Heaven knows! But if you were free today, would you really seek out a girl with no money, no property—a girl whose inheritance is a debt-ridden sheep station about to be claimed by the bank? Would you really choose a girl who could bring nothing to the pursuit of profit that now drives your life? Ted, if you want, I release you from our engagement. I release you with a breaking heart, for the love of the man you once were.'

He was about to speak when she went on:

'This may give you some pain for a short time, but it will only be for a short time. It will be quickly swallowed up in the greater, golden dream you now chase. I only hope you may be happy in the life you've chosen.'

With those words she stood up and walked quickly from the room.

'Spirit!' cried old Scrooge, 'show me no more! Take me home. All you're doing is torturing me.'

'There is one more shadow scene yet to visit. One more!' exclaimed the Ghost.

SWIMMING AWARD

Harri
Huang Jones - Evans

Has Achieved the following swimming award/s

10 m

At a cost of £2.00 for each badge and certificate.

Please return this slip with the money so that we know which certificates to issue.

'No!' protested Scrooge. 'Not one more! No more. Just take me home.'

At this the Ghost took hold of both his arms, held him tightly and turned him around to view the scene that was now unfolding, in a different house, at a different time.

It was a very ordinary room, not big, not flash. There were Christmas decorations around the room, and Christmas cards on top of the bookcase. Sitting in an armchair in shorts and a T-shirt was a pretty young girl. At first Scrooge thought it was the same young girl, that it was Beth. But Beth entered the room—still attractive, but middle-aged now. And the girl was Beth's youngest.

Then Scrooge knew the room for what it was: part of the bank manager's flat above the bank building in the town of Geebung, just one stop down the line from Dandaloo. As he watched, younger children poured into the room. They were Beth's grandchildren, and they laughed and ran, and climbed all over her. Then they ran around the room like a bunch of soldiers on a search-and-destroy operation. Beth just laughed and told them to calm down, and said they wouldn't find their presents because they were too well hidden.

Soon the mother of this wild gang of children arrived with her husband, both bearing armloads of gifts wrapped in Christmas paper to place under the Christmas tree that stood in the corner of the room. Beth got ice blocks out of the fridge for the children, and told them to run downstairs and play in the yard for a while.

They were about to do so when the door burst open and Beth's husband came in, full of greetings and smiles and also bearing armloads of presents.

'More!' said Beth in mock horror. 'Where are we going to put them all? And the children will be spoiled rotten.'

'Well, if we can't spoil them at Christmas, when can we spoil them?' said the jolly middle-aged man. 'Besides which, what's the point of having grand-children if you can't spoil them?'

By this time the children's mother was getting frantic, running around after her unruly brood and trying to stop them dropping their ice blocks on the furniture or on the floor. One more attempt was made to drive the ankle biters out into the backyard for a while. This time it succeeded, and the adults were able to sit down, put their feet up and relax for a bit.

As Beth went to the kitchen to put the kettle on for a cup of tea, her husband called out, 'Beth, I saw an old friend of yours today.'

'Who?'

'Guess.'

'Don't tease me, Dennis—who was it?'

'Well, I had to drive up to Dandaloo in the middle of the day on business. Does that give you a clue?'

'Either tell me now or else no cup of tea for you,' she said with a laugh from the kitchen.

'It was Ted Scrooge!'

'Ted!'

'I passed his office window and saw him at his desk, with his head down, working away. They say his partner, Jack Marley, is lying on the point of death. But there was Ted, still in the office, still working away. He's quite alone in the world now, I hear.'

'Spirit,' said Scrooge in a hoarse voice, 'take me away.'

'I told you,' replied the ghostly Phantom at his side, 'that these things are merely the shadows of the past. They are what they are; they were what they were. They cannot be changed. And don't blame me for what you see.'

'But I can't bear to see them any longer.'

As he turned towards the Ghost to argue with it, Scrooge found that he was back in his own bedroom—his own dark bedroom in the middle of the night.

'Now leave me!' he hissed. 'Just go away. Haunt me no longer.'

As the Ghost did not move immediately, Scrooge grabbed the old Akubra that sat on the chair in the corner of his bedroom and threw it over the head of the Spirit Being, quenching the laser-like light that shone from there.

With the light extinguished the Ghost seemed to shrink and diminish. Summoning up his courage, Scrooge leapt forward and jammed the hat down tightly. He was surprised to find that it seemed to sink into the ghostly substance. Either that or the Ghost was melting beneath it. Scrooge pressed down harder and harder, and slowly the Ghost shrank until Scrooge found he was pushing the hat down toward the floor. And then it was on the floor, and all that was left of the Ghost was a faint glimmer of green light from beneath the broad brim.

Soon even that was gone. Cautiously, Scrooge lifted the old Akubra. It was just a hat. And underneath it was just floor. Scrooge straightened up and threw the hat back onto the chair. Then he suddenly discovered he was tired. No, he was exhausted, and irresistibly drowsy.

He collapsed onto his bed and sank immediately into a deep sleep.

The Third Verse:
The Ghost of
Christmas Present

Ted Scrooge woke up from his heavy sleep with the feeling that so often accompanies such a waking—the feeling of rising up through the waters of a deep pond. As his mind bobbed to the surface he suddenly knew that he was about to hear the town hall clock strike one once more. How he knew, or where this certainty came from, he couldn't have told you.

He sat upright in bed and looked around. Then he pulled up his pillow to support his back and leaned against the bedhead. This time, thought Scrooge, I'll be ready.

He drew his dressing gown more closely around his narrow chest and blinked into the darkness of his bedroom, waiting for the first, faint glimmer of light—the first hint that the next Spirit was arriving. He remembered Jack Marley's words: the first two are due at one o'clock in the morning, and the third at midnight. This time he wouldn't be taken by surprise.

As a businessman Scrooge had often boasted that

he was ready for anything. He prided himself on weighing up every situation and every opportunity in the blink of an eye—in fact, a good deal faster than he could blink his eyes. He was famous for hearing a deal proposed, perhaps a little uncertainly, by a farmer in financial difficulties, and immediately slamming his fist on his desk with a cry of 'Done!' before the poor man had a chance to reconsider. As the iron returned to Scrooge's soul, he told himself he wouldn't be caught napping again. In the darkness he summoned up all his firmness of resolve and determination. Let anything come—from a kangaroo to a crocodile—and he would be prepared for it.

Now, being prepared for anything is not the same as being prepared for nothing. The town hall clock chimed one—a single, deep, resounding 'dong'. Nothing happened. The sound faded away in a slow, dying note. Still nothing.

Scrooge began to tremble. Was there a dark, invisible ghost hovering beside his bed? He felt nothing and heard nothing, and nothing was more unnerving than a dozen ghosts.

That was when he noticed the dim, red glow creeping into his room. What did it mean? Scrooge had heard of cases of spontaneous human combustion—was he about to burst into flames? Then he realised that the glow was coming from the cracks around the doorway. He couldn't remember closing the door. When had he done that? And where was the glow coming from? Was the rest of the house in flames?

Scrooge leapt out of bed, pushed his feet firmly into his slippers and hastily shuffled to the door. Placing his hand on the doorknob, he took a deep breath and threw the door open. Immediately a commanding voice called his name: 'Ted Scrooge! Come in!'

Scrooge obeyed—and found himself in his own bedroom. How could that be? He had just stepped out of his bedroom, and now he was stepping into it. Scrooge grabbed the door frame to steady himself. All right, take a deep breath, he thought; you're standing in the doorway of your bedroom facing inwards, not outwards. However it had happened, it had happened.

It was definitely his own bedroom, there was no doubt about that. But it was strangely changed. Every inch of the walls seemed to be hung with Christmas bush and Christmas decorations. Standing in the corner, in a brightly painted terracotta tub, was a flowering gum tree hung with sparkling tinsel and twinkling lights. The old fireplace in the corner that had not been lit in years was lit now—in fact, it was blazing. And there was a barbecue grill over the glowing coals, and on the grill were sausages and steaks sizzling and spitting.

Facing that barbecue was an armchair—but a most unusual armchair. It was composed of Christmas puddings, and Christmas cakes, and barbecued chickens, and roast turkeys, and legs of ham, and mountains of fresh salad, and cans of beer, and bottles of wine and soft drink, and toys and gadgets and gifts of every description—all with tags showing them to be Christmas gifts. There were strangely shaped objects wrapped up in Christmas paper along with bottles of nuts, trays loaded down with sweets and nibbles, and baskets of cherries, and mangoes, and grapes, and apples, and oranges.

And seated in this strange armchair, sprawling like an old-time king upon his throne, was a jolly Giant.

'Come in!' he repeated, catching sight of Scrooge in the doorway. 'Come in! I think you and I should get to know each other a little better.'

Scrooge inched forward. This was not the bold, determined Scrooge of a few moments earlier. He now felt shrunken and small before this lordly figure. And although there was a smile and a sparkle in the eyes of the Giant, Scrooge didn't care to look directly into them.

'I am the Ghost of Christmas Present!' boomed the Spirit. 'Look at me!'

Scrooge did so. The ghostly Giant was clad in a garment not unlike Scrooge's own dressing gown, except that on the Spirit it looked more like a rich robe. It shone with the glowing green of good pasture after a season of rain, and it was decorated all over with sprigs and leaves of wattle, waratah, banksia, bottlebrush and countless types of bush flowers that Scrooge could not even begin to name. The Giant's face, arms and chest were deeply tanned and weather-beaten, as though he had been working in the bush for many months. He vast feet were bare. He had a beard—a rich, thick, brown, curly beard. This was a continuation of the thick, brown hair that covered his head. And this head wore no decoration except for a sort of wreath that had been woven out of Christmas bush and decorated with kangaroo paw flowers.

The eyes gleamed, the voice was cheerful and the Spectre seemed barely able to contain an abundance of jovial energy.

'A bit different, eh?' laughed the Giant. 'Never seen anything like me before, I reckon.'

'C-c-crikey, no,' stuttered Scrooge. 'Never.'

'You've never met any of the other members of my family? One of them pops around every year, you know. You've never happened to bump into one?' asked the Phantom.

'I don't think so,' said Scrooge. 'It's bottle-tops to Bondi I'd remember if I'd bumped into one of you blokes before. You come from a big family, do you?'

'There are more than two thousand of us.'

'Blimey! Two thousand! Great galloping goannas—that's a lot of mouths to feed.'

The Ghost of Christmas Present stood up.

'Spirit,' said Scrooge, quietly and politely, 'take me wherever you're supposed to take me. Last night I got dragged around against my will. But I learned a lesson from it that has made me a different bloke. So tonight I'm all yours. If you've got anything you reckon you can teach me, then get to it. I'll pay attention, I promise.'

At these words the Ghost of Christmas Present picked up a large stick of timber that had been lying in its lap and thrust it into the fire. As the flame caught, he pulled it back and held it over his head as bright, blazing torch. The Spirit turned to Scrooge and said, 'Touch my robe!'

Scrooge reached out and grabbed a good fistful of that glowing, green garment. Christmas puddings, Christmas cakes, barbecued chickens, roast turkeys, legs of ham, cans of beer, cherries, mangoes, grapes, apples, oranges—all vanished in a moment. So did the room, the fireplace, the barbecue, the glow of light and the hour of the night, and they stood on a street corner in Dandaloo on Christmas morning.

The air was still and dry, and already the sun was blazing down as the oven of the day began to warm up. A few people were out brushing away the fine, red dust deposited on Christmas Eve from their doorsteps and garden paths, or from the cars that stood in the street.

The dust had given a slightly red colouring to every house and building in town. Already doors and windows that had been opened to let in the cool night air had been closed to keep out the rising temperature. The sky was clear blue, without the faintest hint of wispy white cloud that might have promised some relief from the relentless heat of an outback summer. It was a dry, parching heat that seemed to suck the moisture out of the very leaves of the trees. The town dogs were already lying very still on verandahs or under the mottled shade of gum trees. There was nothing very cheerful about such oppressive, energy-draining heat.

And yet an air of cheerfulness somehow filled the street as if it were a bright, fresh spring morning. For as people wandered onto their front verandahs in ones and twos, they called out to their neighbours 'Merry Christmas!', and their grins were large and friendly.

'Come over for a beer when ya get a minute.'

'Try and stop me.'

'What did the mother-in-law give ya . . . socks and hankies again?'

'Whaddaya think! Some things never change.'

And they laughed.

There were children, small children, who ran in and out of the houses—sometimes their own houses, sometimes their neighbours'. Tucked under their arms were the toys they had found with their name on under the Christmas tree that morning. Some of these were flying toys, and soon the buzzing sound of a model aircraft could be heard. A small boy ran past, trying to get a kite to take off in the still air.

'Jim, come inside and help get the kids ready for church,' a woman's voice called from one of the houses.

From open kitchen windows drifted the smells of Christmas dinners beginning to bake—dinners that would be left to their own devices while families hurried off to church. Already the single bell on the wooden post in front of the Dandaloo Community Church was ringing.

Families from properties came driving into town in utes and trucks that banged and clanked and rattled. They parked in the main street and walked towards the old, white, weatherboard church building. Townsfolk left their front doors in straggling, untidy groups, children rushing ahead, parents ambling slowly behind. The kids were in shorts and T-shirts, the women in summer frocks, the men in slacks and open necked shirts (the week before the town minister had announced a total ban on the wearing of ties on Christmas Day).

Inside the church all the windows were open and ceiling fans were slowly revolving. But women still fanned themselves, and men dreamed of the cold drinks that were waiting for them afterwards. Soon the sound of carols could be heard, sung with a tuneless, cheerful enthusiasm.

Afterwards cups of tea were served on trestle tables in the church yard—for country folk still believe that hot tea is good for you on a hot day. And there were free slices of Christmas cake handed around, and some people gave others last minute Christmas cards they'd forgotten to post.

One boy, who had been given a magic set for Christmas, was going around saying, 'Pick a card, any card, don't show me what it is ...' The teenagers shooed him away because the girls were busy talking to the boys and the boys were busy talking to the girls. It was the white-haired grandparents who took the time to let him do his magic trick for them—and who took the trouble to look very astonished at his cleverness.

Slowly, almost reluctantly, the group in front of the church broke up and people made their way back to their houses. Large numbers of relatives assembled at the homes of whoever had volunteered to hold this year's Christmas 'do'. Families from the outlying properties didn't drive back out to their stations, but drove instead to the homes of their friends and relatives in town where they'd been invited to spend the day.

The Ghost led Scrooge onto a deep, shady verandah where they could peer through a large front window. Inside, grandparents were sunk into armchairs, small children were crawling around the floor, and those in between were standing around talking. Everyone had a cold drink in his or her hand, and the teenage son and daughter of the house had been ordered to hand around the trays of sweets and nibbles. These they carried from person to person, trying not to step on the toddlers crawling around on the floor.

Then one of the men came into the room carrying a tray and, with lots of jokes and laughs, topped up everyone's glasses. A couple of the women finished their drinks and made their way out to the kitchen to help with 'serving up'.

One small boy had been given a water pistol for Christmas, but the victims of his watery attacks didn't seem to mind.

'In the face, Neddy,' cried one uncle. 'See if you can get me in the face.'

Neddy rose to the challenge and hit the offered target. Then the uncle who had been the bullseye leant back in his chair and said, 'Ah, that's much cooler.'

But it wasn't much cooler for the town of Dandaloo. In fact, the air was hotter and stiller than ever as the sun climbed higher and the hands of the town hall clock crept towards midday.

From next door came the sound of a raised voice: 'David! You take that yo-yo outside before you break something. Go on! I won't tell you again!' Young David stepped out onto his front verandah, still keeping his yo-yo sawing up and down. He was immediately followed by his younger sister, who kept saying that it was her turn now. While this dispute continued, from the backyard of that same house the smell of onions sizzling on the barbecue was already wafting out into the street.

Scrooge saw that clusters of people were going this way and that as folk hurried from their own homes to the homes of whichever friends or relatives had offered to host this year's Christmas lunch. A few of them drove but most walked, for Dandaloo was a small township. As they walked they laughed and chattered, and they all carried baskets (except for those who carried Eskies or trays with a tea towel draped over them), for everyone was contributing to the feast. Men who'd worn slacks to church had now changed into shorts, and so had many of the women. The adults wore sandals or thongs on their feet while the children were mostly barefoot.

Around each laughing, chattering group ran the family dog, scampering around their ankles and looking up adoringly at each face—for family dogs become just as excited by family celebrations as anyone else. In addition, they had smelled every delicious odour as the food was prepared, and they were looking forward to the generous scraps they would feast on when the lunch was over.

Scrooge then found himself in front of the town's nursing home where two cars were just pulling up. Out of these cars piled the young Salvation Army officer and his helpers—all carrying baskets full of Christmas goodies for the old folk who were bed-ridden. The younger members of the party carried guitars and other instruments, a sure sign that carols would be sung as the food was served.

The Ghost of Christmas Present then whisked Scrooge down the street and around the corner to the church hall. There he saw the town minister and his wife, and the church elders and their wives, and half a dozen other volunteers, serving out their regular Christmas lunch for the poorest, loneliest residents of Dandaloo. The generous spread on which these poor folk feasted was paid for by the citizens and businesses of Dandaloo. Even here the note was one of good fun and jollity. There were streamers and decorations everywhere, and a constant babble of chatter and laughter.

And at every place they visited—every kitchen, every barbecue, every groaning table—the Spirit sprinkled some sparks from his blazing torch onto the food and drink.

'Is there a particular flavour that you sprinkle from your torch?' asked Scrooge.

'There is. My own.'

'Would your flavour enhance any dinner on this day?' asked Scrooge.

'Any kindly given and shared in love. A poor one most of all.'

'Why a poor one most?' asked Scrooge.

'Because it needs it most.'

'But Spirit,' said Scrooge, after a moment's thought, 'don't you cause half of the world's ills? Don't you cause half of the suffering and poverty in the world?'

'Me!' cried the Spirit.

'You are, after all, the Spirit of a religious holiday, and isn't religion the source of much division and unhappiness in this world?'

'There are people who do their deeds of passion, pride, ill-will, hatred, envy, bigotry and selfishness in the name of religion. But they are strangers to me. They don't know me, and I don't know them. Remember what the Founder of this Feast, the one born on the first Christmas Day, once said: "By their fruits you will know them." Remember that, and blame their actions on themselves, not on me.'

Scrooge promised that he would; and they went on, invisible as they had been before, through the small township. As they moved, Scrooge noticed a remarkable ability the Ghost had, that despite his gigantic size he could fit himself into any place with ease. He stood under a low roof, or in a small room, as gracefully and as much at home as in a grand dining room.

Then, with a chuckle and a grin and a sly look in his eye, the Spirit led Scrooge, still grasping his robe, to the modest house of Scrooge's own clerk. As the two unseen visitors floated towards this small fibro dwelling, the Spirit sprinkled sparks from his torch over the corrugated iron roof so that the whole house was filled with the Spirit of Christmas. On the threshold the Spirit stopped to sprinkle sparks on the modest cottage a second time. Scrooge watched open mouthed. Think of that! He knew what a small salary Bob Cratchit had (well, what other sort of salary would Scrooge pay?), and yet here was Bob's little house with a double dose of the Christmas Spirit!

They passed inside and saw Mrs Cratchit, Bob's wife, dressed in her best (even though it was far from new) and bustling around the house. She was preparing lunch, assisted by her daughter Belinda. Son Peter's job was to check the potatoes boiling on the stove with a fork, and with a great sense of responsibility he was determined to do it properly. Two smaller Cratchits, the twins (a boy and a girl), were running around Peter's ankles, making it as hard as possible for him to do his job.

'Martha should be here by now,' fretted Mrs Cratchit. Martha had stayed behind after church to help with the Christmas lunch for the needy in the church hall, and her delay was the reason the Cratchits were having a later than usual lunch that Christmas Day. Martha worked as a maid and assistant housekeeper way out on distant Buckinbar

Station, so the family saw little of her and looked forward to her presence at lunch.

Just then the front door burst open and Martha skipped in. 'We had so many people this year,' she gushed. 'More than last year—and that's why I'm late. Where's Dad?'

'He's out in the backyard bowling to Tiny Tim. Tim found a cricket bat with his name on it under the Christmas Tree this morning.'

'Now,' said Martha, 'what can I do to help?'

'You sit down,' insisted her mother. 'You've just been working your fingers to the bone helping to feed the needy. You have a rest. Belinda and I have lunch well in hand.'

'And me!' added Peter.

'Yes, and Peter,' agreed his mother. 'Peter is on potato patrol this Christmas.'

Just then they heard the fly-screen door leading to the backyard bang.

'That'll be Dad,' said Belinda to Martha. 'Quick! Hide and give him a surprise!'

Martha leapt behind the kitchen door and pulled it half closed so that she couldn't be seen.

As she did this Bob Cratchit walked in, carrying Tiny Tim on his shoulders—for Tiny Tim had an iron frame on one leg, and carried a small crutch.

'We had the most wonderful game of French cricket, didn't we, Tim?' said Bob as he lowered the boy to the floor. Then he looked around and said, 'Where's Martha?'

'Can't come,' said Mrs Cratchit was a straight face, while Belinda could barely suppress a giggle. 'She was called back to Buckinbar Station to help with their big Christmas dinner.'

'What? Our Martha not here for Christmas Day?' spluttered Bob, full of indignation—for the game of French cricket had been a vigorous one, and his adrenalin was pumping.

Martha couldn't stand such a wail of disappointment, so she pushed back the kitchen door and with a laugh threw herself into her father's arms. Tiny Tim flung his small arms around their legs and joined in the hug.

'Come along now, Tim,' said Mrs Cratchit, 'you need a wash before lunch. Belinda, you make sure the other children all wash their hands.'

'And how did little Tim behave?' asked Martha when her father finally released her from his welcoming hug. 'I saw all of you in church, but I came in late with the Buckinbar mob, and the church was so crowded I couldn't get across to you.'

'Tim was as good as gold,' said Bob, 'and better. Somehow he gets thoughtful, spending so much time sitting still rather than running around playing, and he thinks the most unexpected things. He told me as we were coming out of the church that he hoped the people saw him there, because he was crippled, and it might encourage them to remember, on Christmas Day, who it was who made lame beggars walk and blind men see.'

Just then they heard the step-thump, step-thump of Tiny Tim and his crutch on the wooden floor and changed the subject. Bob turned to the important task of making the Christmas punch. In the largest bowl he could find, he mixed up chilled pineapple juice and some freshly squeezed oranges and lemons from the trees in their own backyard, along with some tinned passionfruit and a bottle of dry ginger ale. He added a whole tray of ice cubes then carried the bowl into the family room for later, bearing it before him like a royal courtier carrying the king's crown.

Then the whole family gathered around the big kitchen table, spread with the whitest tablecloth you ever saw. Bob carried Tim to his special place at one corner of the table, then lifted the roast chicken out of the oven onto the carving plate. This he put in the middle of the table and began to carve. Meanwhile, Mrs Cratchit made the gravy, Peter mashed the potatoes, Belinda served up the baked pumpkin and the peas, and Martha prepared the custard for dessert.

All the while the twins ran around the kitchen with cries of 'I'm hungry' and 'Isn't lunch ready yet?'

But eventually it *was* ready, and everyone gathered at the table and filled their plates. Bob gave thanks and they all tucked in to the meal they'd been looking forward to since last Christmas Day.

Finally, every scrap of mashed potato and peas and baked pumpkin was gone, every skerrick of chicken had been eaten, and not even a smear of gravy was left. Then Mrs Cratchit rose to look at the Christmas pudding, which had been bubbling away in its saucepan on the stove for the past hour, while Martha joined her to stir the custard.

'Some may prefer a barbecue outside, or a cold salad on account of our hot weather,' declared Bob, 'but for myself I much prefer a good old-fashioned Christmas feast.' It must be admitted, however, that as he said this his forehead glistened with sweat, and he had used his large white handkerchief at regular intervals during the meal to mop his brow.

Belinda took this as a cue to check that all the windows were open, in the hope that any slight breeze that might stir on that baking hot day would be invited in to cool them just a little.

Then the pudding was served. And what a pudding! Everyone had before them a plate with a generous slice—dark, rich and sweet—filled with dates, raisins, sultanas, fruit and nuts, and swimming in an ocean of thick yellow custard.

'I do declare, dear,' said Bob to his wife after taking his first mouthful, 'your Christmas pudding gets better every year. Better every year!'

This provoked a chorus of approval from around the table, followed by a period of serious silence while everyone ate and enjoyed the climax of the feast.

When the meal was finally over, the dishes were stacked in the kitchen sink and it was universally agreed that the washing up could wait until later. Then the whole Cratchit clan trooped into their small front family room. Because it was shaded by the front verandah on one side and a large gum tree on the other, it was at present the coolest room in the house. And waiting for them there was a bowl of mixed nuts and Bob's big bowl of Christmas punch.

From this they filled their glasses—and a mixed lot of glasses they were, having mostly begun life as Vegemite or jam jars. With the nuts passed around and the glasses filled, Bob proposed a toast:

'A Merry Christmas to us all. God bless us!'

Which all the family re-echoed.

'God bless us every one!' said Tiny Tim, the last of all.

He sat very close to his father's side, squeezed

into the old, worn armchair on which Bob sat. And Bob held his small hand as if he wanted to be reassured that Tim was still there and hadn't been taken from him.

'Spirit,' said Scrooge in a hushed voice, 'tell me if little Tim will live.'

'I see an empty place,' said the Ghost, 'at the kitchen table, and a crutch without an owner, carefully kept in memory of the small boy who used it. If these shadows remain unaltered by the Future, the child will die.'

'No, no,' said Scrooge. 'Oh no, kind Spirit! Tell me he'll live.'

'If these shadows remain unaltered by the Future, no other member of my family will ever see him,' replied the Ghost.

'Dead—before next Christmas?' said Scrooge softly.

'Man,' said the Ghost, 'if man you be in your heart and not stone, will you decide who lives and who dies? Perhaps, in the sight of heaven, you are more worthless and less fit to live than millions like this poor man's son. You're moved by the one you see, yet cold as ice towards the millions you don't see.'

Scrooge looked at the ground, ashamed before the Ghost's sharp words. But he looked up again when he heard his own name spoken.

'Mr Scrooge!' said Bob. 'I give you Mr Scrooge, the man who financed our feast!'

'Who financed our feast, indeed!' cried Mrs Cratchit, looking even hotter under the collar (if that were possible on this scorching Christmas Day). 'I wish he was here! I'd give him a piece of my mind to feast on!'

'Now darling,' said Bob, 'the children! Christmas Day!'

'How can we celebrate Christmas—peace on earth and good will—by drinking the health of such an odious, stingy, tight-fisted, mean-spirited, unfeeling man as Ted Scrooge? Don't look at me like that, Robert—you know him better than anyone else ... you poor fellow.'

'My dear,' said Bob gently, 'it's Christmas Day.'

'I'll drink his health for your sake,' said Mrs Cratchit, 'and for the Day. Long life to him! A Merry Christmas and a Happy New Year! He'll be very merry and happy, I have no doubt!'

The children then joined in the toast. But it was the first thing in that whole day in the Cratchit household that had no real enthusiasm about it. And for a full five minutes it was as if a dark shadow had been cast over the party.

But the shadow passed and the family was then happier than ever. The children played with their Christmas presents, and more nuts and punch were consumed. Bob kept them all amused with silly stories about things that happened at Christmas time when he was a boy, and Martha talked all about life on a big sheep station like Buckinbar.

Peter and Belinda were made to tell everyone about how the last year had gone at school for them, and what they expected of the year to come. On hearing this, the twins began shouting that next year they were going to 'big school'. And while Bob sat in his old armchair, Tim fell asleep in his arms with a smile on his face—for it was Christmas Day, and it was a very happy day for the Cratchit family.

There was nothing great about these events,

nothing dramatic, nothing special, nothing that would make an episode of a television soapie or a reality show. But it was reality nonetheless: the ordinary, warm, happy, sometimes noisy reality of a small family coping as best they could with the demands of life.

The Spirit turned and led Scrooge away, scattering a few last sparks from his torch as they left. Scrooge's eye was on the sleeping figure of Tiny Tim until the last.

The sun was now setting, and a baking hot day was becoming a hot, still, oppressive evening. Once more clusters of people moved up and down the streets of Dandaloo—for some folk were having lunch at one house and dinner at another. The smaller children were already tiring and being carried in their parents' arms. The teenagers stopped to talk to each other on the way—the boys boasting and the girls giggling.

In fact, so many people were on the street that you might have thought there could be no one in any of the houses to expect them or welcome them. But the houses were still far from empty. Those who had served up traditional Christmas lunches were now pouring into their backyards, lighting up their barbecues, and organising easy evening meals of sausages and salads.

And now, without a word of warning from the Ghost, they stood upon the wide, flat saltbush plain. Close by could be heard the rustle and murmur of cattle that had been settled for the night. Just ahead was the glow of a campfire.

'What place is this?' asked Scrooge.

'A drovers' campfire—drovers who must be on the

road with a mob of cattle on Christmas Day, instead of home with their families. And they're here because of that last minute deal you pushed through in late November—the deal that required early delivery. Do you remember?'

Scrooge said nothing, but he nodded. Then he and the Ghost of Christmas Present drew closer, in their invisible way, to the fire and the men gathered around it. The men had their collars turned up and their hats pulled down over their weather-beaten faces, for out here a hot wind was blowing, and sand and dust were in the wind. The oldest man in the group used a stick to lift the billy off the campfire and pour himself another mug of strong, black tea. To this he added a fistful of sugar and a nip of rum.

As the others helped themselves to more tea, the old man took a sip to wet his whistle and then began to sing. In a voice that seldom rose much above the wind on that saltbush plain, he sang them a song about Christmas. It was a song that told the story of the first Christmas. It had been an old song when he was a boy—and from time to time the other men joined in on the chorus.

The Spirit did not stay but, telling Scrooge to take a tight grip on his robe, sped on. In the darkness Scrooge was alarmed to see the pounding waves of the ocean below him. Ahead was a lighthouse—a solitary lighthouse on an island that was little more than a pinnacle of jagged rock, whipped by a storm coming off the Great Australian Bight.

Through the thick, stone wall of the lighthouse Scrooge and the Spirit passed effortlessly. Inside was a solitary man. For a while he moved around checking the various mechanisms. Then he sat down to a meal that he had obviously taken some time and care to prepare for himself from canned meat and vegetables. As he ate his meal and sipped on a glass of red wine, he took from a drawer a bundle of letters from his wife and proceeded to reread each one.

In this silent and solitary scene, with the storm raging outside, Scrooge was surprised to hear a hearty laugh. It was a much greater surprise when he recognised the laughing voice as belonging to his nephew. He turned around and saw that he was now on the brightly lit back verandah of his nephew's house. As well as the usual verandah lights there were strings of coloured lights, and along the full length of the verandah a Christmas crowd was gathered—in a very casual way. Some were sprawled on deck chairs and some leaned back on rickety cane chairs. All of them were coping with the oppressive heat by holding a cold can in their hands from which they took regular sips.

'Ha-ha-ha-ha!' laughed Scrooge's nephew. 'Ha-ha-ha!'

If you happen to know anyone who has a happier, more infectious laugh than Scrooge's nephew (which is most unlikely) then let me know, because his laugh was good-natured and good-humoured and highly contagious. And when Scrooge's nephew laughed, then Scrooge's niece (by marriage) laughed as well. And their friends on the verandah quickly caught the bug and joined in.

'And ... and ...' said Scrooge's nephew, trying to stop laughing so he could speak, 'and he said Christmas was humbug! Honestly he did!'

'Well, he should be ashamed of himself, Steve,' said Scrooge's niece. She was very pretty, this young woman—very pretty indeed—with dark hair and dark eyes.

'Well, he's a funny old fellah,' said her husband. 'He's not as nice as he might be. But that's his way, and I won't say anything against him.'

'And I suppose there's one thing to be said *for* him,' hinted Scrooge's niece. 'He's very rich. At least, that's what you tell me, Steve.'

'But so what?' laughed Scrooge's nephew. 'His money's of no use to him at all. He doesn't do any good with it. In fact, he doesn't do anything with it all.'

'Except make more money,' added Scrooge's niece.

'Exactly,' agreed Scrooge's nephew. 'I don't know what'll happen to it when he dies. Perhaps he's made a will and left it all to the cats' home. I reckon he might want the pleasure of knowing that we'll never get *our* hands on it!'

At this he laughed some more and took another sip of his beer. You never before saw any young man in the world so relaxed about not being rich.

'Well, I have no patience with old Ted Scrooge,' observed Scrooge's niece. And Scrooge's niece's sisters, and the other women at the Christmas party, all agreed.

'Oh, I have!' said Scrooge's nephew. 'I feel sorry for him. I couldn't be cheesed off at him if I tried. Who suffers from his sour growling and grumbling? He does—more than anyone else. He gets it into his noggin to dislike us, and turns up his nose at having Christmas dinner with us. And who misses out? He does! Mind you, I reckon it wasn't much of a dinner he missed.'

'It was a very good dinner!' cried Scrooge's niece, either not noticing or choosing to ignore the sly smile on her husband's face when he spoke those last words. And everybody else at the party joined in to support Scrooge's niece and howl down her husband as 'an ungrateful wretch'.

This produced more howls of laughter, especially from Scrooge's nephew, who turned to one of the other blokes and said, 'What do you reckon, Tony? Do you reckon these young wives of today know how to cook?'

Tony had clearly got his eye on one of Scrooge's niece's sisters, so he immediately shot back that a bachelor like himself was a wretched, lonely outcast who had no right to express an opinion on the subject. At this Scrooge's niece's sister (the plump one with the honey-blonde hair and the big, blue eyes, not the thinner one with the reddish hair and the very full lips) blushed.

'Keep going, Steve,' said Scrooge's niece. 'This husband of mine never finishes a sentence. You were in the middle of saying something about Scrooge.'

'All I was saying was that the result of him having a down on us is that he misses out on our little parties. Which I suppose doesn't do him much harm. I'm sure, though, that he'd have more fun here than locked up in his thoughts, all by himself, or in his mouldy old office surrounded by his dusty account books. And I intend to keep on asking him to call in and see us and join us for a meal—whether he likes it or not—because I feel sorry for the old humbug. He can hop up and down about Christmas as if he's got a bindi-eye in his foot, but I'll still turn up at his office every year, with a big smile on my ugly face, inviting him to Christmas dinner with us. I'll give him a big grin every time I step into his old office and say, "G'day, Uncle Scrooge—how are you?" All he can do is growl at me. And who knows, it might soften him up enough to leave his clerk a couple of hundred dollars in his will. That'd be something. And you know, I think I shook him up a bit yesterday.'

'Good for you, Steve!' said one his mates, and everyone laughed at the idea of Scrooge being shaken up by an invitation to Christmas dinner. But it was thoroughly good-natured laughter.

Then one of the young blokes got out a guitar and began to sing some old Slim Dusty songs—because this was the bush and that was what they liked to sing. One of his mates pulled a mouth organ out of his shirt pocket and joined in, and the others sang along. When the two-man orchestra moved on to 'I Love to Have a Beer with Duncan', Steve interrupted them with shouts of 'Hold on, hold on—I know this one.' He ran into the house, returned with a tin whistle he'd played in the school band and joined in the tune.

Then they switched to a John Williamson song, and everyone laughed when their lead singer couldn't quite remember the words of 'Old Man Emu'.

When he'd run right through his entire repertoire they switched to playing games. These were mostly word games because everyone was too hot to move around much. They played 'Animal, Vegetable or Mineral' (and everyone noticed that Tony pulled his chair closer to the plump sister and whispered clues in her ear when it was her turn to guess). Each person in turn had to think of something and say if what they were thinking of was animal, vegetable or mineral (or a mixture). The company then had to guess what they were thinking of, and ask questions to get more information—but the answers could only be 'yes' or 'no'.

Scrooge himself became so involved in the game that although he was unseen and unheard by them, he kept shouting out his own guesses and questions.

When it was Scrooge's nephew's turn, he told them he was thinking of an animal. He was then exposed to brisk-fire questioning which resulted in him agreeing that it was a live animal, a rather disagreeable animal, a savage animal, an animal that growled and grunted sometimes, that talked sometimes, that was to be found in the Dandaloo shire, that walked about the streets, that wasn't put on display, that wasn't led by anyone with a collar and lead, that had never been put on sale in the saleyards, that was not a horse, or a camel, or a cow, or a bull, or a bear, or a dog, or a chicken, or a pig. And at every question and answer the nephew roared with laughter.

Finally the plump sister (of all people) squealed, 'I know! I know!'

'So what is it?' challenged Steve.

'It's your Uncle Scro-o-o-o-oge!'

Which it was. The plump sister was congratulated by everybody (especially Tony, who was very warm in his congratulations). But some protested that when they asked 'Is it a bear?' the answer should have been 'yes', because a negative answer directed their thoughts away from Ted Scrooge.

'Well, Uncle Scrooge has given us all a good laugh

tonight,' said Steve, 'and it would be mean of us not to drink a toast to him. So I give you the toast: "Uncle Scrooge!" '

And everyone else lifted up their cold cans and chanted, 'Uncle Scrooge!'

'A Merry Christmas and a Happy New Year to the old bloke, wherever he is—and whatever he is!' said Scrooge's nephew. 'He wouldn't accept my Christmas best wishes but he'll have them all the same. Merry Christmas, Uncle Scrooge!'

Uncle Scrooge was so moved by all this that he would have made a short speech in reply, if he'd been able, and thanked them all for their good wishes. But the whole scene vanished on the last word spoken by his nephew, and he and the Spirit were off again on their travels.

The rest of that Christmas night they travelled far and saw much—and the Spirit seemed to bring improvement wherever he went. He stood beside sick beds and they felt more cheerful; beside folk far from their families and they felt closer; by struggling single mothers and they had more patience. In hospitals, in prisons, in every place he visited, the Spirit left a little of his blessing.

It was only one night, but it was a long night; and as it went on, while Scrooge himself was unchanged, he saw that his Phantom Guide was growing visibly older. As they walked out of an army base, the last place they visited, Scrooge noticed that the Spirit's hair was now grey.

'Are spirits' lives so short?' asked Scrooge.

'My life upon the globe is very brief,' replied the Ghost. 'It ends tonight.'

'Tonight!'

'Tonight at midnight. Listen . . .'

Just then the Dandaloo Town Hall clock struck the quarter hour—it was 11.45.

As the chimes were still ringing out, Scrooge said, 'Excuse me if I am being impolite'—he was staring at the Spirit's robe as he spoke—'but there, poking out from the bottom of your robe, is that a foot or a claw?'

'It might as well be a claw, for there is so little flesh on it,' said the Spirit sadly. 'Look!'

From the rich folds of its robe it brought forth two children: wretched, frightful, hideous, miserable. 'Look! Look here! Look, look down here!' exclaimed the Spirit.

They were a boy and a girl. Badly under-nourished, with spindly arms and legs and swollen stomachs, they were at the same time scowling and wolfish. And yet they both knelt, pleadingly, at the Spirit's feet and clung to its robe. Their faces lacked the freshness of childhood; instead they were as wrinkled and withered as if they were very old and close to death. They were not children, but monsters—with a monstrous gleam of greed in their eyes as if they would consume the whole world around them.

Scrooge took a step backwards, startled and horrified. He tried to say they were fine children, but he couldn't make the lie pass his lips.

In the end all he could mutter was, 'Spirit, are they yours?'

'They are Humanity's,' said the Spirit, looking down upon them. 'And they cling to me, appealing from their parents. This boy is Ignorance. This girl is Need. Beware of them both, and of all their kind.'

'Have they no one who can help them? Have they no one to turn to?' asked Scrooge.

In reply the Spirit said, 'They are the government's problem. That's why you pay your taxes.' At the sound of his own words quoted back to him, Scrooge's heart sank as if it were made of lead.

Just then the clock struck twelve.

As the chimes began, the Ghost disappeared, and Scrooge found himself alone again. And when the last of the twelve chimes ended, Scrooge remembered the prophecy of the Ghost of Jacob Marley—that the third Spirit was to come upon the stroke of midnight.

Lifting up his eyes, Scrooge saw a solemn Phantom, draped and hooded, coming like a mist upon the ground towards him.

The Fourth Verse: The Ghost of Christmas Yet to Come

The Phantom slowly, gravely, silently approached. It travelled as lightly over the ground as a wisp of smoke, but something about it suggested that it was heavy—as heavy as dense, ground-hugging fog.

As the shadowy figure, shrouded in gloom, drew nearer, Scrooge found himself trembling; and, partly out of fear and partly to stop them knocking, he fell on his knees.

The Spirit's black cloak covered it completely from head to foot, and the head itself was unseen, hidden in deep shadow inside the folds of the hood. In fact, all Scrooge could see of the ghostly figure was one outstretched hand. It would, thought Scrooge, have been impossible to make out the Ghost in the darkness from which it emerged had it not been for that one outstretched hand.

Scrooge knelt on the ground, still trembling. The ominous figure, tall and stately, stood over him. And even though it neither moved nor spoke, it filled him with deep, heart-chilling dread.

At last he gathered up enough courage, and enough breath, to speak.

'Am I in the presence of the Ghost of Christmas Yet to Come?' asked Scrooge.

The Spirit said nothing, but pointed with its outstretched hand—pointed outwards and onwards, beyond where Scrooge was kneeling.

'Is it your job,' asked Scrooge, his voice faint and trembling as much as his body was, 'to show me what's coming? Will you show me things that haven't happened yet, but that will happen at some time in the future?'

The black hood seemed to shift a little in its folds as if the Spirit had nodded its head. That was the only answer he got.

By this time Scrooge had become quite used to ghostly company, but this silent shape terrified him so much that when he stood up to follow it, he had to force his legs to work—one foot after another, after another.

While Scrooge took a deep breath and gathered his strength, the Spirit paused and turned to look at him. Somehow this made everything worse. Scrooge shivered at the thought that invisible inside the hood's shadow were ghostly eyes that watched him, moment by moment, intently fixed on whatever he was doing.

'Ghost of the Future!' cried Scrooge, 'Wait! Wait! Look . . . to be honest, I'm afraid of you. More afraid of you than of any other ghost I've met in this . . . this really weird experience. I know your visit will do me good and all that. And I'll follow you wherever you want to lead me. But can't you speak to me? Even one word?'

Still it gave him no reply. Still the pale, spectral hand pointed onwards.

'All right then,' said Scrooge. 'All right. You'd better lead on. The night won't last for ever, and I now understand that time is precious. Yes—time is more precious to me than I'd ever realised.'

At these words the Phantom glided onwards. Scrooge followed closely, stepping into its shadow, and when he did so it was as if that shadow lifted him upwards, floating him and the grim Ghost together over the town.

Sights and sounds swirled around him as Scrooge passed from the present moment into the (as yet) unknown future. Daylight sprang up around them. It was a blazing summer's day in the main street of Dandaloo. Still the Spirit carried Scrooge onwards—both of them invisible to passers-by. The Ghost stopped at the saleyards at the edge of town.

This was a place that Ted Scrooge knew well. He had spent many hours here, talking to the auction-eer, the graziers and the buyers. He knew the timber railings and the familiar animal smells. It was sale day but the sales were clearly over. The last of the animals were being pushed and herded by cattle dogs into the back of large, waiting trucks. The crowd was drifting away to the pub for a 'cold one' after a long, hot afternoon of buying and selling.

The Spirit brought Scrooge to a halt beside a little group of men who were still, it seemed, talking business.

Dave Peters, the auctioneer (a fat man with rolling chins and a loud voice), said, 'No, I haven't got a clue how it happened. All I know is the old bloke's dead.'

'When did he die?' asked a stock agent.

'Last night, someone said.'

'What was wrong with him?' asked a grazier as he stuffed tobacco into his pipe. 'Apart from the fact that he didn't have a heart.'

The others laughed and the auctioneer said, 'But then he never did have a heart, did he?' And they laughed again.

The stock agent chimed in. 'He was as tough as old leather—I thought he'd never die.' And then he added with a yawn, 'What's the old misery done with his money?'

Dave Peters' four chins all wobbled as he laughed. 'Blowed if I know. Probably left it to his own company. All I know is he didn't leave it to me. If he had I'd shout you all a beer.'

They all laughed. 'Now I reckon that's a good idea, Dave,' said the grazier. 'The first round's on you!'

At these words the auctioneer stepped back several paces to lock the door to his office, and then the three men walked slowly towards the main street, in the general direction of the Dandaloo pub.

'I reckon it'll be a cheap funeral,' said the stock agent as they walked. 'At least one of us ought to go. After all, we all did business with the old tight wad.'

'Any volunteers?' asked the grazier.

'I'll go if it includes lunch afterwards,' grinned the auctioneer. 'But no free feed—then no Dave. I have to look after my figure, ya know,' he added, patting his enormous stomach.

'Yes, I noticed you've been putting on a bit of condition,' said the grazier.

'Well, if it's next week I can't go,' said the stock agent. 'I'm down at Geebung all next week.'

'Ah, well, I'll go,' said the grazier. 'I can leave the property to run itself for a couple of days and stay in town with my brother-in-law.'

'I know why you want to stay in town,' said the stock agent, digging the grazier in the ribs. 'Your wife's mother is staying out on your station at the moment, isn't she? So the old bloke tumbling off the twig like that gives you an excuse to stay in town for a few days.'

'Just for that,' said the grazier, 'you can buy the second round!'

And they all laughed again as they entered the pub.

Scrooge turned to the Ghost beside him, looking for some sort of explanation. But the Spirit remained silent, and once again raised its ghostly hand to point at two men meeting on the opposite side of the street. Scrooge hurried to hear what they might say—the explanation might lie here.

One of the men was the postman; the other worked at the farmers' co-op. Scrooge had had many dealings with both over the years.

'How ya goin'?' asked one.

'Still breathin'. Yourself?'

'Fit as a Mallee bull,' replied the first. 'I heard Old Dingo has carked it.'

'Yeah, I heard the same. Hot, isn't it?'

'Well, it's nearly Christmas—gotta be expected. Catch ya later.'

'Yeah. Hooroo!'

And that was it. Not another word. That was their meeting, greeting and parting.

Scrooge couldn't understand why the Ghost seemed to think such trivial conversations mattered. But, he thought, there must be some hidden meaning. He would have to puzzle it out since the Spirit refused to speak.

They couldn't be talking about his partner, old Jack Marley, because his death lay in the past, and this was the future. Nor could he think of anyone he knew, or anyone connected to him, that these conversations might be about. But he did understand that whoever they applied to, there was a lesson here for himself.

What he was waiting for was his future self—the Ted Scrooge of tomorrow—to appear, because he was certain that the behaviour of his future self would make some sense of what he was hearing. Scrooge stood and looked around. He hadn't seen himself at the saleyards, and that was a little unusual. And he was nowhere to be seen on the street—although that didn't surprise him.

Just then the Phantom once more raised its ghostly hand and pointed him onwards. Suddenly they were in the air, travelling many miles in mere seconds. Below them was the road out of Dandaloo, heading west. They followed this swiftly until they found themselves on the outskirts of Bourke.

Here the Spirit dropped a little lower, and Scrooge could see an old ute on the road below them. They followed this rattling, rusty vehicle as it drove into the town and pulled up in front of a shop.

It was a poor looking sort of shop—right at the far end of the street, well out of the main shopping area. The paint was faded and its small window was crowded with such a mixture of objects that it was impossible to tell what sort of business it was in. Whatever its trade was, the jumble of unrelated objects in the window was covered by a thin layer of dust.

Scrooge found himself and his ghostly companion standing just inside the dingy store as the ute pulled up in front and two people got out—a thin, middle-aged man and a plump, middle-aged woman. Scrooge was startled to recognise the woman as Mrs O'Riley, his cleaning lady. And the man looked vaguely familiar too.

The interior of the shop was cramped and cluttered. In amongst the clutter was a small, withered old man with grey hair, who looked to be just as ancient and dust covered as the scrambled mixture of odd objects that filled his premises. As the man and the woman entered, he came out from behind his counter and greeted them.

'Nice to see you again, Mr Crypt. And this lady, I take it, is a friend of yours?'

'O'Riley,' said the woman extending a plump hand to be shaken. The shopkeeper responded with a brief clasp from his own bony paw while he squinted at her short-sightedly through thick spectacles.

'Come out to the back room,' he wheezed. 'It's more comfy—and more private.'

He gestured towards a door behind the counter and ushered his two guests through it. As he did so, he turned over the faded piece of cardboard that hung in the middle of the front door so that from the inside it now read OPEN. He pushed the door bolt home, then followed his two guests.

'How's the undertaker's business, Mr Crypt?'

asked the shopkeeper as he joined the man and woman in the parlour. He had said the small room would be more 'comfy' but he had lied. It was just as cluttered and dusty as the shop itself. There were only three chairs: an ancient, over-stuffed armchair and two straight-backed wooden chairs. Before anyone else could be seated, the shopkeeper hurriedly claimed the armchair for himself and waved his guests towards the old kitchen chairs—for that is what they were.

The tiny room looked exactly like the main shop, with the one difference that in a far corner was a small sink, an electric jug, an open packet of tea bags, a jar of instant coffee (of the cheap 'supermarket's own brand' variety) and several stained and ancient mugs. But the shopkeeper did not at first offer his guests tea or coffee. Instead he rubbed his hands together with anticipation and repeated his question to the man:

'Undertaker's business doing well, Mr Crypt?'

'Death and taxes, Mr Chisel, death and taxes,' replied Mr Crypt as he lowered his thin frame cautiously onto one of the rickety wooden chairs. 'I make money out of the first and pay as little as possible of the second.'

The shopkeeper responded with a wheezy laugh. 'And your friend,' he said. 'Introduce me to the lady.'

'This is Mrs O'Riley, an old acquaintance of mine, and a cleaning lady by profession.'

'And a very respectable profession it is too,' said the shopkeeper, with a dusty cough. 'Gives you many opportunities to "clean up", I'm sure.' Again the rasping chuckle came in response to his own joke. 'Now, I take it you've both got something to show me. Ladies first.'

For the first time Scrooge noticed that both the man and the woman were carrying bundles. The woman's was wrapped in what looked like an old linen tablecloth, and as she unfolded it a strong odour of mothballs wafted out. She threw back the last corner to reveal a pile of cutlery and a few small porcelain objects.

'This is silver,' said Mrs O'Riley firmly. 'Real silver. It was filthy when I collected it from the old bloke's cutlery drawer. Tarnished, like. He never cleaned them properly while he was alive. But I've done them up with the old Silvo and they've come up good as new. They should be worth a bit.'

The shopkeeper leaned forward and picked up a butter knife, then a serving fork. These he held close to his eyes as he examined them in the dim light of the room's single light bulb

'Hmmm,' he said at last.

'What does that mean?' demanded Mrs O'Riley.

'It means you're right, dear lady. These are real silver.'

'See—I told you it was worth taking the cutlery. At least this good stuff,' said the lady to her male companion.

'Unfortunately . . .' resumed the shopkeeper, spinning out the word until it sounded as though it had twenty-five syllables, 'unfortunately, it's not a complete set. That considerably reduces the value.'

'What about these then?' asked Mrs O'Riley, handing over the small pieces of porcelain.

The shopkeeper examined each one closely. 'Rubbish,' he said, putting the first piece aside. 'Rubbish,' he repeated as another got the same treatment. 'Rubbish,' he said a third and a fourth time.

Then he brightened up and said, 'This is Royal Worcester, though. Unfortunately, it's been repaired. See the little crack here where it's been glued? Greatly reduces its value, I'm afraid.'

He thought for a bit longer then pulled a piece of chalk out of his pocket. He turned around to a piece of bare plaster wall behind him. This patch of wall was covered with chalk numbers. It seemed to be the place where the shopkeeper did his accounts. He rubbed an area clean with his sleeve, jotted down some new figures, added them up and wrote the total, which he underlined.

'That's as much as I can offer you, I'm afraid,' he said, displaying his yellowed teeth in what he thought was an ingratiating smile. 'If I offered you any more I'd be robbing myself, honestly I would.'

'That includes the tablecloth?'

'It does.'

A wave of disappointment passed over the woman's face. She glanced sideways at the undertaker. He gave her the very slightest nod of his head.

'All right then,' she said, in a flat tone of voice, 'I'll take it.' Then she added under her breath, 'And you're a bigger thief than I am.'

If he heard this, the shopkeeper tactfully ignored it. 'Now, Mr Crypt,' he said cheerfully, 'what do you have to offer?'

The undertaker unfolded his parcel, wrapped in old newspaper. It revealed a suit, a pair of boots and a wristwatch.

'He seldom wore the suit,' said Mr Crypt. 'Maybe once or twice, that's all. I think he bought it for a funeral a few years back. Probably thought it would look bad if he didn't wear something decent.

Anyway, no one in town ever saw him wear it again. It's been dry cleaned and pressed.'

'And you removed this suit . . . ?' asked the shopkeeper.

'From the man himself. At that moment in time when he was in no condition to resist or comment.'

'So what was he buried in then?'

'A nice, plain shroud. What's the point of sticking a good suit six feet underground? That would be a criminal waste.'

'I quite agree with you,' said the shopkeeper. 'Unfortunately it's a little hard to dispose of clothing at a profit. What else do you have?'

'This wristwatch.'

The shopkeeper took hold of this and held it up to the light. 'Not new,' he commented, 'but not bad. I can let you have a little something for that. What else?'

'These boots,' said the undertaker. 'Genuine R.M. Williams, and almost brand new.'

'Good quality,' agreed the shopkeeper. 'But then, to find a buyer you have to find a man with just those size feet.'

Once again the old man turned around and scribbled some calculations on the wall in chalk. These calculations ended in a number that he underlined.

'That's it, Mr Crypt,' he said. 'That's my first and final offer. Any more than that and I'd have to go out of business.'

'Hand it over then,' said the undertaker bitterly, placing his bundle on the floor.

Scrooge looked at this scene, and listened to these words, with horror. The woman—the woman he'd employed as his cleaner!—was nothing but a thief who stole from her clients after they'd died. And her friend, the undertaker, seemed to be in the habit of robbing corpses. Horrible!

'Well now,' cackled the shopkeeper. 'Our business is done, and I'm happy to put the billy on and offer you a cup of tea or coffee.'

His visitors accepted.

As the old shopkeeper staggered to the sink and turned on the electric jug, he said, 'Well, the old man will never miss these things anyway.'

Mrs O'Riley laughed joylessly and said, 'He frightened everyone away. There was no one there to keep an eye on him or care. All alone he was, at the end.'

'Spirit!' cried Scrooge, shivering from head to foot. 'I get the point! What happened to this poor dead fellah could happen to me. I—good grief, what's this?'

Suddenly the scene had changed and Scrooge was in a bedroom—a bare, plain bedroom. Lying on top of the bed was a person—a person covered from head to toe by a white sheet! The room was very dark, and Scrooge could see nothing that might identify the corpse.

He turned towards the Phantom. Its steady hand was pointed towards the head of the corpse. Scrooge crept closer. The sheet was so carelessly thrown over the head of the deceased that Scrooge thought a mere flick of his finger would pull it back and reveal the face. But Scrooge's hand trembled. He hesitated in fear. Then, drawing upon all his courage, he leaned forward and seized the sheet.

Or at least he tried to. His hand passed right through it. He was, after all, a ghostly visitor to the future. He could touch nothing. He could no more remove the sheet than he could remove the frightening Spectre that hovered by his side.

'Spirit!' he said. 'This is a fearful place. I think I've learned a lesson here, so please, take me away.'

Still the Ghost pointed with an unmoved finger at the covered head of the corpse.

'I understand,' muttered Scrooge sadly. 'I understand. But I can't do it. I've tried and I can't. I don't have the power.'

Again the Ghost seemed to look at him with its invisible, deathly stare.

'Is there anyone,' pleaded Scrooge, 'anyone at all in this town who feels any emotion at this man's death? If there is, then show me, please. Please.'

The Phantom spread its dark robe before him for a moment, like a giant, black bat's wing, and when it withdrew it they were in a different place.

They were on the other side of town.

This was where the poorest houses were to be found—mostly four-roomed fibro shacks. Calling them 'cottages' was applying far too grand a word to them. They were built on small blocks near the creek, cheap land because it was prone to flooding. The shire council had often talked about banning all building on the creek flats, but the problem was the humble homes that were already there. So no action had been taken (although the council had formed a sub-committee to talk about it).

Scrooge found himself transported inside one of the fibro shacks. It stood on the far side of the creek, on twenty-five acres of land. And it was clear that someone had been trying to farm the land as a market garden. It was so small that it could never have been a very profitable farm, but two floods that

Spring—one after the other—had killed even those modest hopes.

In the front room of the fibro farmhouse, which served as kitchen, dining room and sitting room all in one, was a mother with three children. The children, poorly dressed or half naked, played on the floor while the woman, in frayed clothes that should have been discarded long ago, paced back and forth. Every so often she looked up at the clock.

At length the sound of an ancient truck could be heard rattling into the yard and the dogs began to bark. Then the longed-for step was heard on the porch, and she threw open the front door. There stood her husband. He had deep lines of worry in his face although he was still young.

He staggered in and collapsed in a chair.

He was silent, staring at his children playing on the floor.

But she needed to know, so she prompted him. 'Is it good—or bad?'

'Our debt still stands. Our due payment date has not been changed.'

'There's no chance of keeping the farm, then? We're bankrupt?'

'No. There's still hope, Doreen.'

'Only if *he* would give in—give us time—give us one more season. And that would be a miracle.'

'He'll never give in. He's passed that now,' said her husband. 'He's dead. Remember I tried to see him yesterday and was told he was dying? I thought it was just an excuse to fob me off. But it was true. He's gone.'

'So what happens to our debt now? I suppose it doesn't die with him?'

'No such luck.'

'Then who takes it over? Who do we owe the money to now?'

'I don't know. But it will all take time, you see. It will take weeks, maybe months, for the will to go through probate—assuming he's made a will. And the Christmas and New Year holidays are almost here, and that'll slow it down a bit further. I reckon I'll harvest both the pumpkins and the cabbages before we have to make another payment.'

'So we'll be all right, then?'

'We're gonna be okay, sweetheart. Tonight you can get your first good night's sleep in a long time.'

And then his wife did something he hadn't seen her do for many months. She smiled.

This was indeed emotion in response to a man's death, but not the emotion Scrooge had hoped to see. He turned to the Phantom and pleaded, 'Let me see some tenderness, some softer emotions, connected with this death. If you can't show me that then the chill of that death chamber will haunt me forever.'

The Ghost whisked Scrooge across town. As they travelled Scrooge looked about, to right and left, hoping to see himself somewhere. But he failed to catch even a glimpse of his future self. Then the swift journey was over, and they were inside Bob Cratchit's house. There he saw the mother and the children. The woman was stitching something, and the children were sitting at the table doing a jigsaw puzzle.

And they were quiet. Very quiet.

At length Mrs Cratchit put down her work and said, 'Your Dad ought to be home by now. This is the time he's usually here.'

Peter, who was reading a book quietly in the other corner, said, 'Past his usual time. But he walks a bit slower than he used to, I've noticed.'

'I remember,' said his mother, in a hushed voice, 'when he walked with Tiny Tim on his shoulders, very fast.'

'Yes,' said Peter. He wanted to say more, but couldn't think of what else to say.

The children at the table turned to look at their older brother and their mother. One looked as if she was about to add her voice in agreement, but then seemed to decide that it was better to say nothing.

'He was very light to carry,' resumed their mother, in a voice barely above a whisper. 'And Dad used to say he was no trouble at all—no trouble at all. Ah, there's your Dad at the door now.'

She hurried to meet him, and then told him he was looking peaky and he should sit down while she put on a cup of tea. When he sank into his favourite armchair the two smallest Cratchits, the twins, ran over and climbed onto his lap, one on each knee.

His wife came back with the tea and said, 'You went then, did you, Robert?'

'I promised him I would. As often as I could.'

He drank his tea in silence for a time. Mrs Cratchit busied herself in the kitchen, getting the dinner. Peter went back to his book, and the twins climbed down and went back to their jigsaw puzzle. Bob sat lost in thought, sipping his tea. Finally, when the cup was empty, he did what they knew he would do, what he did every day. He went out to the back room.

It was a very small bedroom—an enclosed end of the verandah. But weatherproof and snug and very comfortable, for Bob had made it that way. He sat down in the chair beside the small bed where he had often read to Tim. The toy cars were still lined up on the window sill, and the books Tim used to draw pictures in were still on the bedside table.

After a while he felt better again, and Bob came back out to the kitchen. The others were gathered around the big table and Mrs Cratchit was serving dinner.

'Just a salad today,' she was saying. 'But it's such a hot day it seemed the sensible thing.'

As they ate, Bob told his family about the extra-ordinary kindness of Mr Scrooge's nephew.

'He ran into me in the street today, and he said that I looked ... just a bit down. You know. And he asked what had happened. So I told him. And he shook my hand and expressed his deepest sympa-thies, and he asked to be remembered to you, dear. He said, "Please say how deeply sorry I am to your good wife." And, by the way, however did he know that?'

'Know what, dear?'

'That you were a good wife.'

'Everyone knows that!' said Peter.

'Quite right!' cried Bob. 'Anyway, he went on to say that if he could ever be of help to me, or anyone in the family, in any way, I wasn't to hesitate to get in touch. And he wrote his phone number and address down on a bit of paper—I've got it here somewhere.'

As this point Bob searched all his pockets until, at last, he triumphantly produced the note. He imme-diately rose from the table and put this small but valuable piece of paper on the mantelpiece. Then he resumed his seat and went back to eating.

However, after one more mouthful he stopped again to say, 'Oh, yes, and he said that he thinks he knows where he might be able to help Peter get an apprenticeship.'

'Unreal!' said Peter grinning, who had just finished his final year at school and was looking forward to doing some real work (much more interesting than school work), and possibly bringing home enough money so he could help his family a bit.

'And you know what Tiny Tim would have said,' continued Bob. 'He would have said, "God bless him!" And he would have meant it! We won't ever forget Tim, will we, kids?'

'No, never, Daddy,' said one of the twins as she reached out and patted her father's hand.

'You're a wonderful family,' said Bob. 'All of you. And I'm very proud of you.'

Scrooge observed all of this with a lump in his throat and a kind of fluttering knot in his stomach. Then he turned to the Ghost and said, 'Spectre, I have a feeling that my time with you is nearly over. I don't know how I know it, but I know it. But before you go, tell me: who was that man we saw lying dead?'

The Ghost of Christmas Yet to Come conveyed him in the same mystical way as before, although Scrooge thought at a different time: indeed there seemed to be no order in these future visions. They seemed to be jumbled up somehow. The only thing that connected them was that they were part of the Future.

Their swift, shadowy travel took them past the town and its busy and not-so-busy occupants. They passed Scrooge's house.

'I know this house!' cried Scrooge. 'It's mine! So what shall I be doing here in the days to come?'

By way of reply the Spirit pointed onwards—and they resumed their strange journey. For just a moment they passed the front window of the office of *Scrooge and Marley—Stock and Station Agents*. Scrooge glanced in and saw that things were different. There was different office furniture—newer furniture. And the man sitting at the main desk was not himself.

Still they whisked silently onwards, until they reached the town cemetery. Here they came to a stop. It was a hot summer's evening, but the sun was low in the west and the shadows were long. The Phantom pointed at a particular grave site. Scrooge walked slowly forward in the purple twilight, stumbling occasionally in the semi-darkness.

At last he reached the grave the Spirit was pointing at. It was a neglected plot—overgrown with weeds. The shabby headstone was covered in moss and lichen. And while one grave nearby, the smallest grave, had fresh flowers placed upon it, this grave had nothing.

Scrooge turned to the Ghost and said, 'Before I look any closer, tell me this. These things I have seen, are they things that *must* be? Or are they only things that *might* be?'

The Ghost remained silent and unmoving, and continued to point downwards at the grave and the plain headstone. Scrooge inched forward and bent over to read the name.

Just then a slight breeze moved the branches of the gum trees that lined the western side of the cemetery. In the flickering, mottled, blood-red light of the setting sun scattered through the leaves, Scrooge read the name on the headstone: EDWARD SCROOGE.

'Oh, no,' he cried as he sank onto his knees. 'Am I that man in that death chamber?'

He looked up. The Phantom still towered over him. 'Listen! Listen, Spirit!' he said, clutching tightly at its black robe. 'I'm not the man I was. I've been changed by everything I've seen. Why show me this if my case is hopeless?'

For the first time the Ghost's hand appear to quiver just a little.

'Good Spirit,' whimpered Scrooge, 'take pity on me. Tell me ... tell me that it doesn't *have* to be like this. Tell me it can be different. Tell me I can have another chance—a chance to be a very different man.'

The ghostly hand trembled.

'I will honour Christmas in my heart, and I will keep its spirit alive every day of the year. I will honour and serve the One who gave us Christmas. I will live as Marley said I should: loving God with all my heart, all my soul and all my strength, and loving my neighbour just as much as I love myself. And I will live in the Past, and the Present and Future. And the Spirit that made the First Christmas shall remake me.'

In his agony Scrooge reached out and grabbed hold of that cold, spectral hand. The Phantom tried to pull away, but Scrooge hung on more tightly still. And still the Phantom pushed him back and tried to free its hand.

In his desperate prayer and awful struggle, Scrooge opened his eyes and saw that the Phantom's cloak and hood had become his own crumpled sheets, and that the hand he was holding so tightly was his own bedside clock.

The Final Chorus: The End of It All

Yes! His bedside clock! And they were just sheets—his own sheets! This was his bed, and his bedroom. Scrooge felt his arms, his legs, his chest, his face. Then he leapt out of bed, turned on the light and looked in the mirror on the front of his old wardrobe.

Yes, it was really himself—and he was *alive*! That meant he had time, time that lay before him, time in which to do things.

'And I will live in the Past and the Present and the Future!' said Scrooge to himself over and over again. 'And the true Spirit of Christmas shall strive within me.'

Staring at his figure in the mirror, he muttered to himself: 'Oh, Jack Marley! Good old Jack Marley! Heaven and Christmas Time be praised for this! Oh, Jack—what a good bloke to send me this warning!'

He had been weeping in desperation in his struggle with the Ghost of Christmas Yet to Come, and his face was still damp with tears. His hands fumbled as he pulled off his dressing gown and the clothes he had been wearing. He hurried into the bathroom for a quick shower and a shave (this last was quite risky because his hands were unsteady). Then, still trembling all over, he pulled on clean clothes.

All the time he kept mumbling and laughing to himself, 'I don't know what to do. But I do know I want to do something ... something different ... to *be* different.'

Then a thought occurred to him, and he rushed out of the room to the linen cupboard and looked inside. There was his best tablecloth, the Irish linen one his mother had bought, still packed away in its mothballs. From there he ran to the kitchen and threw open the cutlery drawer: all of his tarnished old silver cutlery was still there. His best suit was still hanging in his wardrobe, he'd put on his new R.M. Williams boots and his wristwatch, and the porcelain ornaments were still in the places they had always been.

'None of it has happened! All those awful things I saw in that future vision haven't happened!' At this he laughed: a loud, genuine, happy laugh. And for a man who was so out of practice he did it very well. This first cheerful laugh was followed by several more.

Then he pulled himself together and looked at his kitchen door.

'That's the door the Ghost of Jack Marley walked through,' he said, 'and over there is the window he left through—and that I saw the wandering Spirits through.' Hurrying back into his bedroom he threw open the front window, saying, 'And this is the window the Ghost of Christmas Past took me through with a leap. It's all here! It's all true! It all happened!'

Suddenly he thought of something: 'I don't know what day of the week it is. I don't know how long I've been off among the Spirits!'

Just then Scrooge saw a small boy running down the street, trying to get a brand new kite into the air on that hot, still morning.

'Boy! Boy!' Scrooge called through his open window.

The boy stopped and walked slowly and hesitantly onto Scrooge's front lawn. He was cautious because all the kids in the street knew what a grouch old Scrooge was. They all made fun of him behind his back, but they were afraid to go near him when they saw him.

'Boy!' called Scrooge again. 'What day is it?'

The boy looked puzzled. He and his mates always knew that Scrooge was as balmy as a bush turkey, but now it seemed that he'd finally gone right round the twist. But he thought it better not to say this to Scrooge.

'It's CHRISTMAS DAY,' he replied simply. And his tone of voice implied, 'It's blinkin' obvious, you old goat. Even you oughta know that!'

Scrooge drew his head back in the window and chuckled to himself. 'Christmas Day! Christmas Day! I haven't missed it after all! The Spirits have done it all in one night. They can do anything they like. Of course they can. Of course they can.'

Scrooge almost ran back to his kitchen, and from its hiding place behind the dinner plates he pulled out the rusty tin in which he kept his ready cash. He emptied the tin and stuffed all of its contents into his pockets. He had never carried so much cash on his person before. The old Scrooge would have thought it foolish and dangerous, but the new Scrooge just wanted to get on with celebrating Christmas.

Thus cashed up, Scrooge hurried out of his front door. (And although he remembered to close it, for the first time in his life he forgot to lock it.) On his way out he ran his hand over the doorknob that had shown him the face of Jack Marley and muttered, 'Dear old doorknob! Dear old doorknob!'

Down the street he went at a pace he hadn't made his old legs move for many years. Already the sun was blazing down and a boiling hot Christmas Day was on its way, but Scrooge was oblivious to the heat.

At the top of his street he turned the corner and hurried towards the shops.

As he bustled past front fences he called out to folk on their verandahs, 'Merry Christmas!'

They were left feeling bewildered.

'Wasn't that old Scrooge?'

'I thought it was. But he said "Merry Christmas"! He always was a weirdo, but strike me pink, his brain must have finally gone completely bung!'

Small children he passed had their heads patted by Scrooge and a dollar thrust into their hands. They examined these coins suspiciously. If Scrooge was giving money away, then there must be something wrong with it!

Finally, he arrived at Charley Carlton's butcher's shop. But he didn't knock on the closed front door. Instead he went around the side, because the butcher and his family lived behind the shop.

His persistent knocking finally brought Charley himself to the side door.

'Good morning, Mr Scrooge—' he began.

'Merry Christmas!' cried Scrooge, thrusting out his hand.

Charley shook this offered hand warily, saying, 'And a Merry Christmas to you too, Mr Scrooge. But look, I can't do anything for you today. The shop's closed—it's Christmas Day.'

'I know, I know,' said Scrooge. 'I should have done all this a long time ago—a *long* time ago. Now, Charley, I won't drag you away from your family or ask you to do any work. But would you have, in your cold room, a ham and a turkey you could let me have? I'll pay you double the usual price, and all I ask is that you get them out of your cold room and hand them over.'

As he spoke Scrooge began pulling money out of his pocket.

'Well … I suppose so,' said Charley cautiously. 'Come in, I'll have a look.'

Charley let Scrooge in and led him into the parlour. As he crossed the room, Scrooge said 'Merry Christmas' to Mrs Carlton (who looked puzzled and surprised) and all the little Carltons. Each of the children got a pat on the head and a dollar as Scrooge passed through.

They entered the shop and Charley opened his cold room door. He turned on the light.

'Big ones, mind you,' said Scrooge behind him. 'The biggest ham and the biggest turkey you can find.'

A minute later the butcher turned around and displayed to Scrooge a large ham and a large turkey.'

'These do?' asked Charley.

'Fine. Fine. I'll take them with me,' said Scrooge. 'How much?'

The butcher named a price. Scrooge thrust a fistful of money into his hand and said, 'Keep the change.'

The butcher put the ham and the turkey in the biggest carry bag he could find and handed it over to Scrooge—who then left the way he had come, with many mutterings of 'Thank you, thank you, Merry Christmas, Merry Christmas', over and over again.

Back on the street in the heat of the Dandaloo sun, Scrooge found himself standing on the corner with a carry-bag full of ham and turkey tucked under his arm, uncertain as to what he'd do next. He hadn't planned all that far ahead.

But just at that moment he saw the town's one and only taxi cruising down the street towards him. He waved frantically. Bert Hitchens, the owner and driver, wanted to ignore his signals, but seeing Scrooge was one of the town's richest men he thought better of it and pulled over. But he only stopped to apologise.

'Sorry, Mr Scrooge,' said Bert, winding down the driver's window. 'I'm not working today. It's Christmas Day. I'm on my way to my sister's now to pick her and the kids up and take them back to my place for Christmas lunch.'

'This will only take a few minutes, Bert, only a few minutes, I promise you. And I'll pay you very well for it.'

Bert was sceptical. He knew what Scrooge's 'pay very well' meant—the minimum payment and a miserly tip. But before he could say no, Scrooge had opened the passenger's door and dropped a large shopping bag on the front seat. At the same time he thrust into Bert's hands more cash than Bert had ever seen Scrooge handle before—let alone hand over to someone else.

'Just take this bag to Bob Cratchit's house, will you? Do you know where that is? And will that be enough money?'

With a dazed expression on his face the taxi driver nodded and said, 'Yes.' Scrooge closed the passenger's door and shouted, 'Off with you then. And Merry Christmas, Bert!'

Bert put his foot to the floor before (he thought) the old dingo came to his senses and changed his mind. He could drop off the bag at Bob's on the way to his sister's place—it would only take him three minutes out of his way.

Behind him Scrooge stood on the footpath thinking of what Bob Cratchit, and Mrs Cratchit, and all the little Cratchits would make of the meal that came in a taxi. It was such a delicious idea that Scrooge chuckled to himself over and over again.

At that moment the church bell began to ring.

'The church bell!' cried Scrooge to himself. 'Ringing in Christmas Day! It really is Christmas Day!'

Off he went to church. There he greeted everyone with a warm handshake and a hearty 'Merry Christmas!' The town minister seemed surprised but delighted, and was about to say that it was a long time since he'd seen Scrooge in church when he seemed to think better of it and said only, 'And a Merry Christmas to you too, Mr Scrooge.'

During the service Scrooge sang the carols (which he now thought of as those dear, lovely, old Christmas carols) more heartily than anyone. And the shire clerk, who took up the offering, saw with amazement how much money Scrooge put in the plate (although Scrooge tried to slip the notes out of his hand as surreptitiously as possible). And then during the sermon Scrooge listened more closely and paid more attention than anyone else in church that day.

Afterwards he stayed and mingled. Scrooge had never been known to mingle ever before. But on that day he mingled. He accepted his cup of tea and slice of Christmas cake with pleasure and many words of thanks. When a small boy who didn't know his fearsome reputation approached and wanted to do a magic trick, those standing nearby waited for Scrooge to grumble and growl and snap the boy's head off. But it didn't happen.

'Pick a card, any card,' said the boy. 'Don't show me what it is. Don't tell me what it is. Memorise it. Now put the card back in the pack.'

Scrooge obediently did as he was told.

'Shuffle the cards,' said the boy.

Scrooge shuffled the cards.

'Now, tell me,' said the boy, 'the name of your card.'

'The three of hearts,' said Scrooge, grinning with delight at the whole procedure.

'Now pull out the third card from the top of the pack,' said the boy with the supreme confidence of a ten-year-old.

Scrooge pulled out the third card, turned it over and exclaimed with astonishment (which was genuine if slightly overacted), 'Well, blow me down! Look at that! The three of hearts! How on earth did you do that?'

And the small boy grinned with pleasure, while onlookers shook their heads in disbelief and muttered things about Scrooge having had 'a touch of the sun'.

After church Scrooge set off at a brisk pace to walk to his nephew Steve's house. On his way he passed the young Salvation Army officer with his band of helpers delivering their Christmas hampers. Scrooge rushed over to the young man and thrust the remaining contents of his left-hand pocket (which was a lot of money) into the startled man's hands.

'Mr Scrooge!' exclaimed the young man.

'Sorry about the other day,' muttered Scrooge. 'Come back to my office again next week. Tell me about any other community projects you have in mind, and let's work out some arrangement for regular giving.'

With that Scrooge turned around quickly to cover his own embarrassment and resumed his brisk walk.

On reaching his nephew's house he paced back and forth past the front door a dozen times before he had the courage to go up and knock. Finally he made a dash and did it.

'Uncle Ted!' cried Scrooge's nephew upon opening the door. 'This is a—well, to be honest, this is a surprise. But it's a pleasure as well, Uncle Ted. I'm delighted you changed your mind.'

And Scrooge's nephew's wife was just as surprised when Scrooge was shown through to the back verandah where she was mixing a bowl of punch. And so was the plump sister when she arrived. And Tony when he arrived. And everyone else when they arrived.

But surprise turned to delight as old Ted Scrooge

was warm, and friendly, and happy, and hearty, and joined in every part of the day's festivities. He helped his nephew's wife serve up lunch and then helped her clear away. He helped serve up afternoon tea as well, and helped clear away again.

And when he said he'd imposed on them long enough and it was time he was going, Scrooge's nephew, and Scrooge's nephew's wife, were most insistent that he stay for Christmas dinner as well. So he did. And he joined in every game and laughed louder and more often than anyone else.

When, late that night, Scrooge said that he really must be going as it was getting very late, his nephew insisted that he come back the next day to watch the start of the Boxing Day Test on television with them.

Which he did. In fact, he spent the whole of Boxing Day with them. As they watched the Test from the Melbourne Cricket Ground, they flicked back and forth between that and the start of the Sydney-to-Hobart yacht race. And they lazed around and ate Christmas leftovers, and Scrooge had never before felt more like part of a family.

The next day was a Thursday, and it was a working day. Despite two days of partying Scrooge was determined to be up early so that he could be the first at the office that day. He wanted to arrive early to catch Bob Cratchit coming in late! That was the thing he'd set his heart on.

And he did it: yes, he did!

Scrooge threw himself behind his desk well before nine o'clock and began busily scratching away at an account book. The clock on the office wall struck nine. No Bob. It struck quarter past. Still no

Bob. Scrooge sat facing the front door of the office so that he'd see Bob when he arrived.

It was eighteen and a half minutes past nine when Bob bustled in through the front door, caught sight of Scrooge staring at him and hurried to his own desk.

'Hello?' growled Scrooge in his usual voice—or as closely as he could imitate it. 'What do you mean by coming in at this time of day?'

'Sorry, Mr Scrooge,' said Bob. 'I'm really sorry. I know I'm late.'

'Yes, you are. Step over here to my desk for a moment please.'

As he stepped over Bob pleaded, 'It's just because of Christmas Day and Boxing Day, and I won't let it happen again.'

'I'll tell you what, Mr Cratchit,' said Scrooge. 'I'm not going to stand for this sort of thing any longer. And therefore—' At this point Bob's face went green with anguish. And then his jaw dropped open with surprise as Scrooge leapt up, dug him in the ribs and said, 'therefore, I'm about to raise your salary!'

Bob stared. He edged a little closer to the big, heavy wooden ruler on Scrooge's desk. He thought his boss had gone mad, and if he became violent Bob thought he might have to use the ruler to subdue him.

'Merry Christmas and a Happy New Year, Bob!' said Scrooge, offering his hand.

Bob shook hands and started to grin—still feeling confused, but very pleased and happy at the same time.

'I'll raise your salary, Bob,' continued Scrooge, 'and try to help that little family of yours in any way

I can. And before you start work today, Bob, turn on that electric fan—it looks like we're in for another scorcher. And by the way, would you be so kind as to price an air conditioner for the office—I can't have you sitting through such stifling heat back there any longer.'

Well, Scrooge did everything he said he'd do for Bob's family, and more. He paid for a specialist for Tiny Tim, who did NOT die, and became Tim's honorary Grandfather.

Scrooge became very involved in the township and shire of Dandaloo. He took an active interest in local charities and in the local church. People said they had never known such a generous or jolly old man.

Some people laughed behind his back at the strange alteration that had taken place. Scrooge knew this and thought, 'Let them laugh. If it gives them pleasure, then I'm happy to be the cause of laughter.'

Scrooge had no further contact with Spirits. As far as Spirits were concerned, Ted Scrooge 'took the pledge' and adopted a policy of Total Abstinence from then on.

And everyone who knew him said that Scrooge knew how to keep Christmas better than any man alive. And so, as Tiny Tim observed, 'God bless us, every one!'

The Last Word

When Charles Dickens wrote the original version of this Christmas ghost story back in 1843, he introduced it by saying, 'I have endeavoured in this Ghostly little book, to raise the Ghost of an Idea . . .' And then he said of his readers: 'May it haunt their houses pleasantly . . .'

To those words I can only add a hearty, 'Amen.' Or, as the citizens of Dandaloo would put it: 'Good on ya!'